OpenStack 2025 Cookbook

Second Edition

Modern OpenStack Administration with Flamingo 2025.2, OVN Networking, Terraform Automation, Skyline Dashboard, and Prometheus Monitoring

Jorven Halquin

Published by: GitforGits

www.gitforgits.com

Printed in India

First Printing: March 2026

ISBN: 978-93-49174-28-3

Cover Design by: Kitten Publishing

Disclaimer:

This book, including all its text, diagrams, and illustrations, is an original work developed for educational and informational purposes. The content is not affiliated with, endorsed by, or sponsored by OpenInfra Foundation or any other company, brand, or entity referenced within. All brand names, product names, and trademarks mentioned are the property of their respective owners and are used in a descriptive, educational context only. Every effort has been made to ensure that no copyrighted or trademarked material has been copied or misused in this book. All diagrams and illustrations that are not original have been used with proper attribution and credit to their respective sources.

If you believe that any content in this book infringes upon your copyright or trademark, please contact us immediately at support@gitforgits.com. Upon notification, corrective action will be taken promptly.

Content

Preface

For those seeking practical expertise on OpenStack Flamingo, and the services that drive modern private and enterprise cloud environments, you need look no further. With this book, you gain immediate access to the latest insights on OpenStack 2025.2 Flamingo. This book is for those who want to practically experience how OpenStack works, how its services connect, and how to manage them with confidence in real-world deployments.

Inside, you'll master the core OpenStack services that matter most, such as Keystone for identity, Glance for images, Nova for compute, Neutron and OVN for networking, Cinder for block storage, Placement for resource tracking, Skyline for web-based management, and Gnocchi and Prometheus for monitoring and metrics. I will teach you to manage users, projects, roles, tokens, images, instances, networks, routers, floating IPs, security groups, volumes, and service endpoints. It also covers automation with Terraform, validation, troubleshooting, and operational visibility for a strong and reliable cloud administration.

I strongly recommend this book to cloud engineers, system administrators, DevOps practitioners, architects, and technical learners who want hands-on, production-oriented knowledge of OpenStack Flamingo. Whether your goal is building a lab, improving operational skills, or understanding the architecture behind a modern cloud, this book will show you how to get there. It offers a clear path through the platform's essential services and workflows.

In this book you will learn to:

- Proactively deploy and configure core OpenStack services in a structured, production-focused environment.
- Understand Keystone identity management, including users, roles, projects, domains, LDAP, and federation workflows.
- Build and manage images, metadata, and secure image delivery with Glance and related services.
- Utilize Nova, flavors, hypervisors, quotas, and placement concepts to provision and administer compute resources.
- Construct OpenStack networking using Neutron, provider networks, tenant networks, routers, and floating IPs.
- Implement OVN-based networking with logical switches, logical routers, metadata services, and encapsulation technologies.
- Maximize storage potential with Cinder, streamline volume attachment workflows, and seamlessly integrate block storage strategies.

- Automate OpenStack infrastructure using Terraform for repeatable provisioning, validation, state tracking, and modular design.
- Utilize Gnocchi and Prometheus to proactively monitor cloud health with metrics, exporters, alert systems, and archive policies.
- Identify and resolve common issues with OpenStack services, networking, authentication, and deployment using practical validation techniques.

GitforGits

Prerequisites

Whether your goal is building a lab, improving operational skills, or understanding the architecture behind a modern cloud, this book will show you how to get there. I strongly recommend this book to cloud engineers, system administrators, DevOps practitioners, architects, and technical learners who can get a strong hands-on, production-oriented knowledge of OpenStack in administering their cloud.

Codes Usage

Are you in need of some helpful code examples to assist you in your programming and documentation? Look no further! Our book offers a wealth of supplemental material, including code examples and exercises.

Not only is this book here to aid you in getting your job done, but you have our permission to use the example code in your programs and documentation. However, please note that if you are reproducing a significant portion of the code, we do require you to contact us for permission.

But don't worry, using several chunks of code from this book in your program or answering a question by citing our book and quoting example code does not require permission. But if you do choose to give credit, an attribution typically includes the title, author, publisher, and ISBN. For example, "OpenStack 2025 Cookbook, Second Edition by Jorven Halquin".

If you are unsure whether your intended use of the code examples falls under fair use or the permissions outlined above, please do not hesitate to reach out to us at support@gitforgits.com.

We are happy to assist and clarify any concerns.

Acknowledgement

I owe a tremendous debt of gratitude to GitforGits, for their unflagging enthusiasm and wise counsel throughout the entire process of writing this book. Their knowledge and careful editing helped make sure the piece was useful for people of all reading levels and comprehension skills. In addition, I'd like to thank everyone involved in the publishing process for their efforts in making this book a reality. Their efforts, from copyediting to advertising, made the project what it is today.

Finally, I'd like to express my gratitude to everyone who has shown me unconditional love and encouragement throughout my life. Their support was crucial to the completion of this book. I appreciate your help with this endeavour and your continued interest in my career.

Chapter 1: Setting up OpenStack Flamingo 2025.2

Introduction

The OpenStack is a robust cloud platform, but its successful implementation starts with a well-prepared environment. This chapter will cover the critical initial steps, from preparing the hardware and configuring the operating system to installing and setting up the key OpenStack services. We start with addressing the hardware requirements necessary for deploying OpenStack Flamingo 2025.2. This includes selecting appropriate hardware, and preparing physical infrastructure to support scalable cloud environment.

Next, we will run through setting up Ubuntu for OpenStack. After this, we will practically touch base to the installation and configuration of core OpenStack services, such as Keystone for identity management, Glance for image management, Neutron for networking, Nova for compute resources, Cinder for block storage, and skyline for dashboard. And lastly, we will learn to define and implement network topology. It will include configuring the network components for communication between different OpenStack services and our cloud infrastructure.

Recipe 1: Preparing Hardware for OpenStack Deployment

For our understanding, we will consider an example of GitforGits throughout this book. We are considering it as a fast-growing technology company, that has reached a point where their traditional infrastructure is struggling to keep up with the demands of their expanding operations. And, now to maintain agility and support their growth, they've decided to transition to a private cloud solution. After careful consideration, they chose OpenStack for its open-source flexibility and robust feature set. Now, their goal is to deploy OpenStack on their existing fleet of Linux servers so that, they can manage compute, storage, and networking resources without any discomfort.

So here, we will learn to carefully prepare the hardware on which OpenStack will run. The following steps teaches to prepare the existing Linux hardware to serve as a reliable foundation for the OpenStack cloud.

Hardware Requirements

First, we will assess the hardware requirements for OpenStack deployment as OpenStack typically requires at least two servers. One is for the controller node, and the other for compute nodes.

The given below are the recommended hardware specifications for each node:

Controller Node

- CPU: Minimum 4 cores

- RAM: Minimum 8 GB
- Storage: Minimum 100 GB
- Network: 1 NIC for management, 1 NIC for external access

Compute Node

- CPU: Minimum 4 cores
- RAM: Minimum 16 GB
- Storage: Minimum 100 GB
- Network: 1 NIC for management, 1 NIC for external access

Network Configuration

If we are setting this up, try to have at least two network interfaces on each server so you've got one for management and one for external access. In more complex setups, we might need extra network interfaces for storage and other functions. Once you've done that, go ahead and adjust the settings on each node's network interface. This will make sure everything is connected right, and we will be able to assign IP addresses based on the network architecture you've got in mind.

For GitforGits, it's important to design a network that can handle the anticipated traffic and provide redundancy where needed. And for this, it will be of better value to think about using VLANs or VXLANs to separate network traffic for management, storage, and external access.

In addition, we need to get the following tasks done:

- Set a unique hostname for each node to easily identify them in the network.
- Configure NTP or chrony on all nodes to ensure consistent time across the network.
- Update all installed packages to the latest versions to ensure compatibility with OpenStack.
- Adjust firewall settings to allow communication between nodes on required ports, while ensuring that unnecessary ports are closed for security.

After all this, we have a good and reasonable hardware foundation for deploying OpenStack.

Recipe 2: Setting up Ubuntu for OpenStack Flamingo Installation

The first edition of this book introduced OpenStack Bobcat. What changes now is the latest release, called as **OpenStack Flamingo 2025.2**. The OpenStack release records list **Flamingo** as the **2025.2** maintained release, while **Bobcat** is already marked **End Of Life**. The Ubuntu also documents that Flamingo is available for **Ubuntu 24.04 LTS** through the **Ubuntu Cloud**

Archive.

Preparing Ubuntu Environment

To start with, we begin by refreshing the package metadata, applying the latest updates, and rebooting such that our system starts from a clean and current baseline.

```
sudo apt update
sudo apt upgrade -y
sudo apt dist-upgrade -y
sudo reboot
```

After rebooting, we then disable the swap, as OpenStack services require it to be off for optimal performance:

```
sudo swapoff -a
sudo sed -i '/ swap / s/^/#/' /etc/fstab
```

Installing OpenStack Client

The OpenStack client can manage OpenStack services via the command line:

```
sudo apt install -y python3-openstackclient
```

This client will be used throughout the setup to configure and manage services in the Flamingo release. From this point onward, we will assume the CLI is already available on our controller node and will build our service configuration around that assumption, as we move through Keystone, Glance, Neutron, Nova, and Cinder.

Adding OpenStack Flamingo Repository

First, add the repository for the OpenStack Flamingo release:

```
sudo add-apt-repository cloud-archive:flamingo
sudo apt update
```

This step ensures that we install the latest version of OpenStack services directly from the Flamingo release.

Installing OpenStack Packages

Now, we will install the necessary OpenStack Flamingo packages, focusing on the controller node components:

```
sudo apt install -y keystone glance placement-api nova-api
nova-conductor nova-novncproxy nova-scheduler neutron-server
neutron-plugin-ml2 neutron-ovn-metadata-agent ovn-central ovn-
host openvswitch-switch cinder-api cinder-scheduler
```

These packages include the core services for identity, image management, compute, networking, and block storage.

Configuring Database and Messaging Services

The OpenStack relies on a database and messaging service and for this, we will install and configure MySQL through MariaDB and RabbitMQ.

- MySQL Installation

```
sudo apt install -y mariadb-server python3-pymysql

sudo mysql_secure_installation
```

- RabbitMQ Installation

For this, we need to set a strong password for **root** and remove any unnecessary users by writing the following:

```
sudo apt install -y rabbitmq-server

sudo rabbitmqctl add_user openstack StrongPassword

sudo rabbitmqctl set_permissions openstack ".*" ".*" ".*"
```

In the above code, do not forget to replace **StrongPassword** with a secure password.

Configuring OpenStack Services

Next, we will now configure each OpenStack service to connect to the database and messaging service. For example, in the **keystone.conf** file:

```
[database]

connection =
mysql+pymysql://keystone:StrongPassword@controller/keystone

[oslo_messaging_rabbit]
```

```
rabbit_host = controller
rabbit_userid = openstack
rabbit_password = StrongPassword
```

This above similar configuration we must repeat for all other services.

Starting Services

After configuring, we will now start the services, and we need to ensure that they start automatically on boot too:

```
sudo systemctl restart mariadb
sudo systemctl enable mariadb
sudo systemctl restart rabbitmq-server
sudo systemctl enable rabbitmq-server
openstack --version
apt-cache policy keystone
```

After putting the above commands, we can confirm that the supporting services are running and that the controller node is now sourcing the Flamingo package stream. With these above outlined steps, GitforGits will have the Flamingo release of OpenStack prepared on Ubuntu, with the newer controller package set, OVN-oriented networking components, Placement included, and the legacy Nova and Linux bridge choices removed.

Recipe 3: Upgrading to OpenStack Flamingo 2025.2

Most of us would be running **Bobcat, Caracal, Dalmatian, or Epoxy**, and I want to teach we to move safely to **Flamingo 2025.2** without disrupting workloads. So, in this recipe, we will perform that upgrade step by step, and we will validate each core service at the end so we can confirm that Keystone, Nova, Neutron, Placement, and Cinder behave correctly after the transition.

Pre-Upgrade Health Check

Before we could touch the repositories or packages, we need to verify that the current cloud is healthy. So here, we begin by checking service status and basic API responsiveness using the following commands:

```
openstack service list
openstack compute service list
openstack network agent list
openstack volume service list
```

Each of the above service should report an active or enabled state. Here, we confirm that instances, volumes, and networks exist and are operational:

```
openstack server list
openstack volume list
openstack network list
```

At this point, we are not changing anything. We are establishing a known-good baseline so we can compare results after the upgrade.

Database Backup

Every OpenStack service stores state in MariaDB. The schema migrations will occur during upgrade, so here, we need to take a full database backup:

```
sudo mysqldump --all-databases --single-transaction --quick --
lock-tables=false > openstack_backup.sql
```

This backup protects Keystone identities, Nova instance records, Neutron networks, Cinder volumes, and Placement inventories. We need to store the backup safely before proceeding.

Repository Transition to Flamingo

Our next step is to ensure that the controller node points to the correct repository. If the cloud is running Bobcat, Caracal, Dalmatian, or Epoxy, then the current Ubuntu Cloud Archive entry will reflect that release. Here, we just need to replace it with Flamingo.

To do this, we will first identify the current repository:

```
grep -R cloud-archive /etc/apt/sources.list.d/
```

After this, we will remove the old release pocket:

```
sudo add-apt-repository --remove cloud-archive:bobcat
sudo add-apt-repository --remove cloud-archive:caracal
```

```
sudo add-apt-repository --remove cloud-archive:dalmatian
sudo add-apt-repository --remove cloud-archive:epoxy
```

From the above code, we will remove the one that applies to the current system, and add the Flamingo repository:

```
sudo add-apt-repository cloud-archive:flamingo
sudo apt update
```

With this, the system is now sourcing Flamingo packages.

Stopping OpenStack Services

We will be stopping the OpenStack services before package upgrades. It is much needed to prevent schema inconsistencies during migration.

So here, we will execute the following:

```
sudo systemctl stop nova-api nova-scheduler nova-conductor
sudo systemctl stop neutron-server
sudo systemctl stop cinder-api cinder-scheduler
sudo systemctl stop placement-api
sudo systemctl stop keystone
```

The RabbitMQ and MariaDB will continue to remain running.

Package Upgrade

After this, we will now upgrade the control plane packages to Flamingo versions:

```
sudo apt upgrade -y
sudo apt dist-upgrade -y
```

This will install the Flamingo binaries for Keystone, Nova, Neutron, Placement, and Cinder.

Database Schema Migrations

After packages upgrade, we then need to apply schema migrations for each of the services:

- Keystone

```
sudo keystone-manage db_sync
```

- Placement

```
sudo placement-manage db sync
```

- Nova

```
sudo nova-manage api_db sync
sudo nova-manage cell_v2 map_cell0
sudo nova-manage db sync
```

- Neutron

```
sudo neutron-db-manage upgrade head
```

- Cinder

```
sudo cinder-manage db sync
```

Each of the above commands upgrades the database schema to match Flamingo expectations.

And then later, we will restart the services:

```
sudo systemctl start keystone
sudo systemctl start placement-api
sudo systemctl start nova-api nova-scheduler nova-conductor
sudo systemctl start neutron-server
sudo systemctl start cinder-api cinder-scheduler
```

Here, we need to wait a few seconds to confirm if the **systemd** reports all services active.

Post-Upgrade Validation

We will now move on to validating the cloud thoroughly for all the services as below:

- Keystone Validation

```
openstack token issue
openstack user list
```

Here, a successful token issuance confirms identity service integrity.

- Placement Validation

```
openstack resource provider list
```

The resource providers must appear for compute nodes.

- Nova Validation

```
openstack compute service list
openstack hypervisor list
```

Here, the hypervisors must report up status.

- Neutron Validation

```
openstack network agent list
openstack network list
```

This is very important. The agents must report alive status, and networks should remain intact.

- Cinder Validation

```
openstack volume service list
openstack volume list
```

The volume services must report enabled and up.

And then finally, we need to confirm that the package versions reflect Flamingo:

```
apt-cache policy nova-api
```

The installed version must correspond to the Flamingo release stream.

At this stage, our cloud has moved from Bobcat, Caracal, Dalmatian, or Epoxy to Flamingo 2025.2 successfully.

Recipe 4: Installing and Configuring Keystone

The OpenStack, in general, is designed to control large pools of compute, storage, and networking resources, through a dashboard, command-line tools, or through an API. The OpenStack allows we to deploy only the components that we need for the specific use case.

Following is a brief overview of the core 10 OpenStack components:

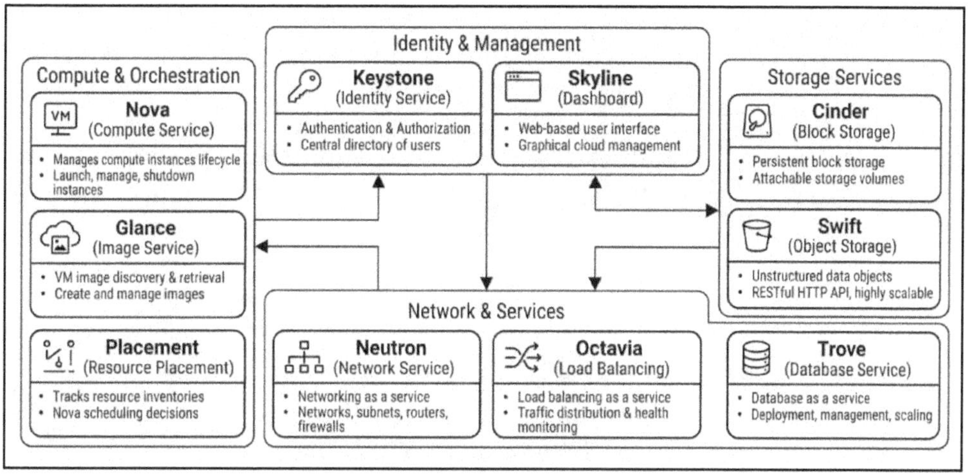

Fig 1.1 OpenStack 2025.2 Components

- **Keystone** manages authentication and authorization for OpenStack services. It provides a central directory of users mapped to the OpenStack services they can access.
- **Glance** handles the discovery, registration, and retrieval of virtual machine images. It allows users to create and manage images that can be used to deploy instances.
- **Nova** manages the lifecycle of compute instances in an OpenStack environment. Nova orchestrates everything from launching an instance, managing its resources, to shutting it down.
- **Neutron** provides networking as a service between interface devices managed by other OpenStack services, typically compute nodes. Neutron manages networks, subnets, routers, and provides advanced features like load balancing and firewalls.
- **Cinder** provides persistent block storage to run instances. Cinder allows we to create and manage block storage volumes that can be attached to instances for data storage.
- **Swift** stores and retrieves unstructured data objects via a RESTful, HTTP-based API. It is highly scalable and designed to store a large amount of data with redundancy.
- **Skyline** provides a web-based user interface to interact with OpenStack services. It allows users to manage their cloud infrastructure graphically.
- **Placement** tracks resource inventories, allocations, and traits so Nova scheduling can place instances on the right compute resources. It provides a dedicated API that exposes resource provider data used during scheduling decisions.
- **Octavia** provides load balancing services for OpenStack workloads, allowing applications to distribute traffic across multiple instances with health monitoring and listener configuration.
- **Trove** provides database management as a service, offering deployment, management,

and scaling of databases.

Understanding Keystone

Keystone is OpenStack's identity management system. It acts as a central directory for all OpenStack services and their users, handling authentication, authorization, and service discovery. The Keystone allows users to authenticate through various methods, including username and password, token-based authentication, and external authentication systems like LDAP.

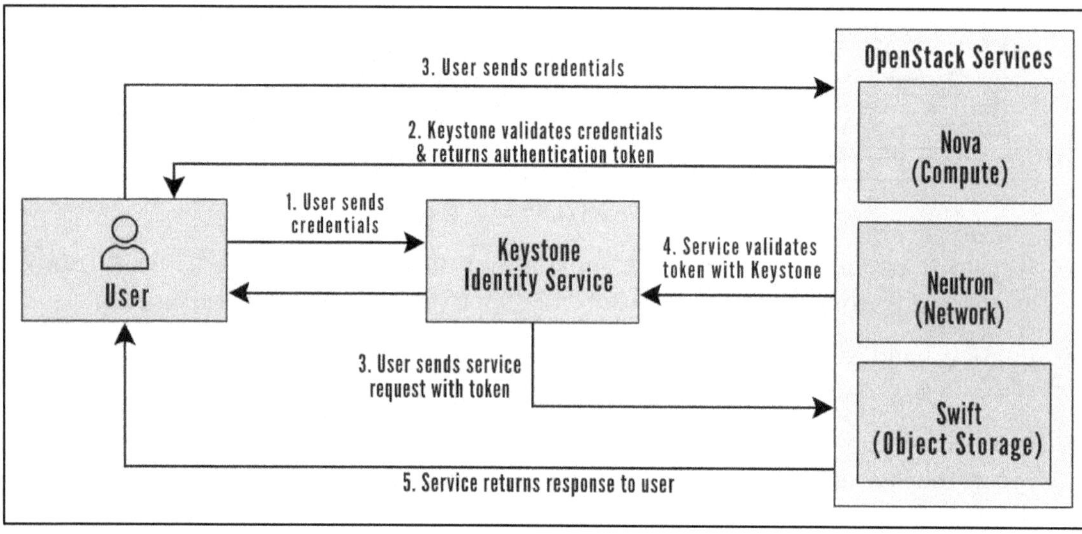

Fig 1.2 Keystone Working Mechanism

Following are the key features of Keystone:

- Keystone can manage multiple tenants (projects) and domains, allowing for isolated environments within the same cloud infrastructure.
- Users can be assigned roles that define what actions they can perform on specific resources within a project.
- It issues and manages tokens that are used by users and services to authenticate and interact with OpenStack APIs.
- It provides a catalog of all available OpenStack services, their endpoints, and regions.

To establish a safe and controllable OpenStack environment, we must first install Keystone. To guarantee that no unauthorized users can access or modify cloud resources, Keystone will act as the authentication backbone. So, let's move on to installing and configuring it on the Ubuntu system running the OpenStack Flamingo release.

Install Keystone Packages

The Keystone can be installed using the OpenStack package repository that was added in the previous recipe:

```
sudo apt update
sudo apt install -y keystone
```

This above command installs the Keystone service along with its dependencies.

Configure Keystone Database

The Keystone requires a database to store its data, including users, roles, and service catalogs. And, commonly MySQL is typically used for this purpose. So, to begin with, we will first create a database for Keystone:

```
sudo mysql -u root -p
```

Once logged into MySQL, we then execute the following commands to create the database and grant appropriate permissions:

```
CREATE DATABASE keystone;
GRANT ALL PRIVILEGES ON keystone.* TO 'keystone'@'localhost'
IDENTIFIED BY 'StrongPassword';
GRANT ALL PRIVILEGES ON keystone.* TO 'keystone'@'%'
IDENTIFIED BY 'StrongPassword';
FLUSH PRIVILEGES;
EXIT;
```

After this, we will then populate the Keystone database:

```
sudo keystone-manage db_sync
```

This above command initializes the Keystone database schema.

Configure Keystone

Next, we will proceed to configure the Keystone service. For this, we will edit the **keystone.conf**.

```
[database]
connection =
mysql+pymysql://keystone:StrongPassword@controller/keystone
```

After this, we then configure the **token** provider. The **fernet** token format is quite popular and recommended for simplicity and security. So, we will use the same format:

```
[token]
provider = fernet
```

Initialize Fernet Keys

The fernet tokens require a key repository to encrypt and decrypt tokens. In the below, we will then initialize Fernet key repository:

```
sudo keystone-manage fernet_setup --keystone-user keystone --
keystone-group keystone

sudo keystone-manage credential_setup --keystone-user keystone
--keystone-group keystone
```

It will create the necessary keys and sets up the repository too.

After this, we then need to bootstrap the Keystone, so that it can create initial configuration for the service:

```
sudo keystone-manage bootstrap --bootstrap-password
StrongPassword \
  --bootstrap-admin-url http://controller:5000/v3/ \
  --bootstrap-internal-url http://controller:5000/v3/ \
  --bootstrap-public-url http://controller:5000/v3/ \
  --bootstrap-region-id RegionOne
```

Configure Apache HTTP Server

Now, the Keystone runs behind the Apache HTTP server. So here, we will now enable the Apache **wsgi** module and restart the service:

```
sudo apt install -y apache2 libapache2-mod-wsgi-py3
sudo service apache2 restart
```

This will confirm to us that Apache is set up very well to handle requests to Keystone.

Create Keystone Domain, Projects, Users, and Roles

Before we start setting up the project, users and such tasks, we must verify if the Keystone is functioning correctly. And for this, we will try exporting the admin credentials:

```
export OS_USERNAME=admin
export OS_PASSWORD=StrongPassword
export OS_PROJECT_NAME=admin
export OS_USER_DOMAIN_NAME=Default
export OS_PROJECT_DOMAIN_NAME=Default
export OS_AUTH_URL=http://controller:5000/v3
export OS_IDENTITY_API_VERSION=3
```

And then, we will try issuing a command to request a token:

```
openstack token issue
```

If the command returns a token, then we can say confidently that the Keystone is successfully installed and operational.

Now that Keystone is up and running, we can begin setting up domain, project, user, and assigning roles:

```
openstack domain create --description "Default Domain" default
openstack project create --domain default --description "Admin Project" admin
openstack user create --domain default --password-prompt admin
openstack role create admin
openstack role add --project admin --user admin admin
```

Populate Service Catalog

Finally, we then populate the Keystone service catalog with available OpenStack services. Here, each service requires an entry in the service catalog so that it can be discovered by other OpenStack components.

For example, to register the Keystone service itself:

```
openstack service create --name keystone --description
"OpenStack Identity" identity
```

```
openstack endpoint create --region RegionOne identity public
http://controller:5000/v3

openstack endpoint create --region RegionOne identity internal
http://controller:5000/v3

openstack endpoint create --region RegionOne identity admin
http://controller:5000/v3
```

We need to follow the similar above steps to register Glance, Nova, and Neutron.

Recipe 5: Installing and Configuring Glance

Within the OpenStack ecosystem, Glance is the service that handles finding, registering, and retrieving virtual machine images. These images are like the templates or "blueprints" that are used to make the virtual machines. Glance is basically a central storage place for these images, and it gives them to other OpenStack services like Nova when instances are launched. The images managed by Glance can be bare-metal images, virtual machine snapshots, or custom-built images that are tailored to specific application needs. It also works with various storage backends, like local file systems, object storage (like Swift), and external storage systems (like Ceph).

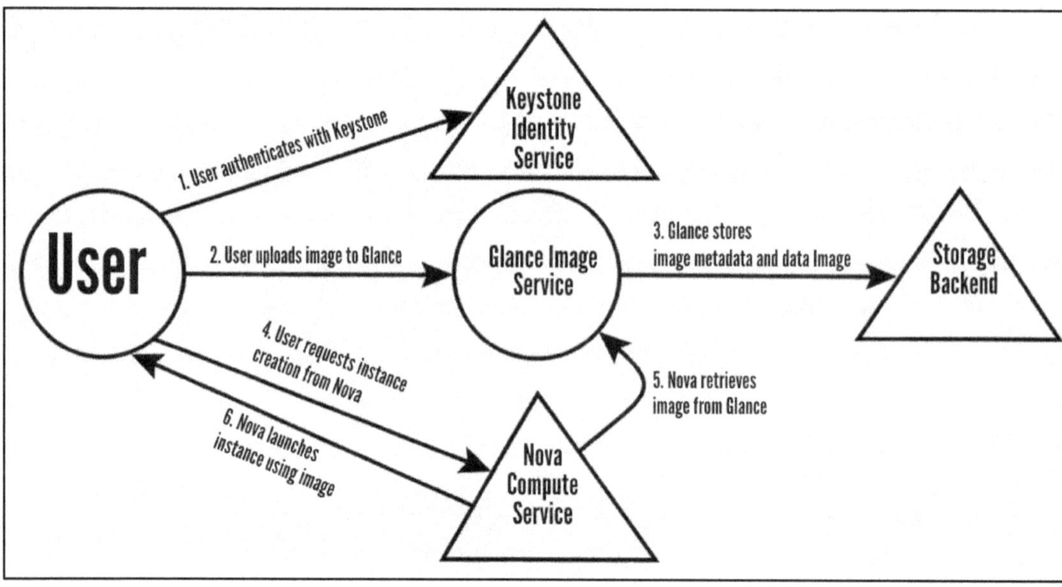

Fig 1.3 Working of Glance

The Glance assists GitforGits by:

- offering single point of control for managing all virtual machine images used within the cloud.

- supporting multiple image formats, such as QCOW2, RAW, VHD, and VMDK.
- allowing to manage different versions of images to track updates and roll back if necessary.
- seamlessly integrating with Nova, Cinder, and other OpenStack services for launching instances or attaching to volumes.

Install Glance and Configure Database

Like Keystone, we will get the Glance service installed on controller node:

```
sudo apt update
sudo apt install -y glance
```

The Glance requires a database to store image metadata. And, like Keystone, the Glance too uses MySQL for this purpose. After getting logged into MySQL, we can execute following commands to create Glance database and grant necessary permissions:

```
CREATE DATABASE glance;
GRANT ALL PRIVILEGES ON glance.* TO 'glance'@'localhost'
IDENTIFIED BY 'StrongPassword';
GRANT ALL PRIVILEGES ON glance.* TO 'glance'@'%' IDENTIFIED BY
'StrongPassword';
FLUSH PRIVILEGES;
EXIT;
```

Next, we then synchronize the Glance database:

```
sudo glance-manage db_sync
```

Configure Glance

We will now configure the Glance service by setting up the database connection in **glance-api.conf** file:

```
[database]
connection =
mysql+pymysql://glance:StrongPassword@controller/glance
```

Next, is to configure the **keystone** authentication settings to allow Glance to authenticate with the Keystone service:

```
[keystone_authtoken]
auth_url = http://controller:5000/v3
memcached_servers = controller:11211
auth_type = password
project_domain_name = Default
user_domain_name = Default
project_name = service
username = glance
password = StrongPassword
```

In the above, we need to specify the storage backend which Glance will use to store images. For simplicity, we'll use the local file system:

```
[glance_store]
stores = file, http
default_store = file
filesystem_store_datadir = /var/lib/glance/images/
```

Now here, we must ensure that the **filesystem_store_datadir** directory is correctly set up to store images.

Register Glance with Keystone

To allow other OpenStack services to discover and use Glance, we shall register the Glance service in Keystone's service catalog.

And for this, we will first create the Glance user:

```
openstack user create --domain default --password-prompt
glance
```

And then, we will assign the **admin** role to the Glance user in the **service** project:

```
openstack role add --project service --user glance admin
```

Next, we will then create the Glance service entry:

```
openstack service create --name glance --description
"OpenStack Image" image
```

And finally, we will create the public, internal, and admin endpoints for the Glance API:

```
openstack endpoint create --region RegionOne image public
http://controller:9292

openstack endpoint create --region RegionOne image internal
http://controller:9292

openstack endpoint create --region RegionOne image admin
http://controller:9292
```

With the above configuration complete, we are well good to start the Glance services:

```
sudo systemctl enable glance-api
sudo systemctl start glance-api
```

Uploading Image to Glance

Our next step is to upload a sample image to verify if Glance can store and manage images. For this, we will use the CirrOS image from the following URL:

http://download.cirros-cloud.net/0.5.2/cirros-0.5.2-x86_64-disk.img

```
curl -O http://download.cirros-cloud.net/0.5.2/cirros-0.5.2-
x86_64-disk.img

openstack image create "CirrOS" --file cirros-0.5.2-x86_64-
disk.img --disk-format qcow2 --container-format bare --public
```

This command downloads the CirrOS image and uploads it to Glance. After the upload is complete, we will list the images again:

```
openstack image list
```

The CirrOS image should now appear in the list, confirming that Glance is properly configured and functional.

Managing Image Metadata

We can now view the metadata for any image:

```
openstack image show "CirrOS"
```

To add or modify metadata, we can use the **--property** flag. For example, to specify that this image is 64-bit:

```
openstack image set --property architecture=x86_64 "CirrOS"
```

With this, the Glance is very well now integrated with Keystone for authentication, and the images can be stored, retrieved, and managed through the OpenStack interface.

Recipe 6: Installing and Configuring Neutron

Neutron is the networking component of OpenStack, responsible for providing "Networking as a Service" (NaaS) between interface devices managed by other OpenStack services like Nova. Neutron offers a powerful, flexible, and scalable networking solution that allows cloud administrators to define and manage networks, subnets, routers, and other networking services such as firewalls, VPNs, and load balancers.

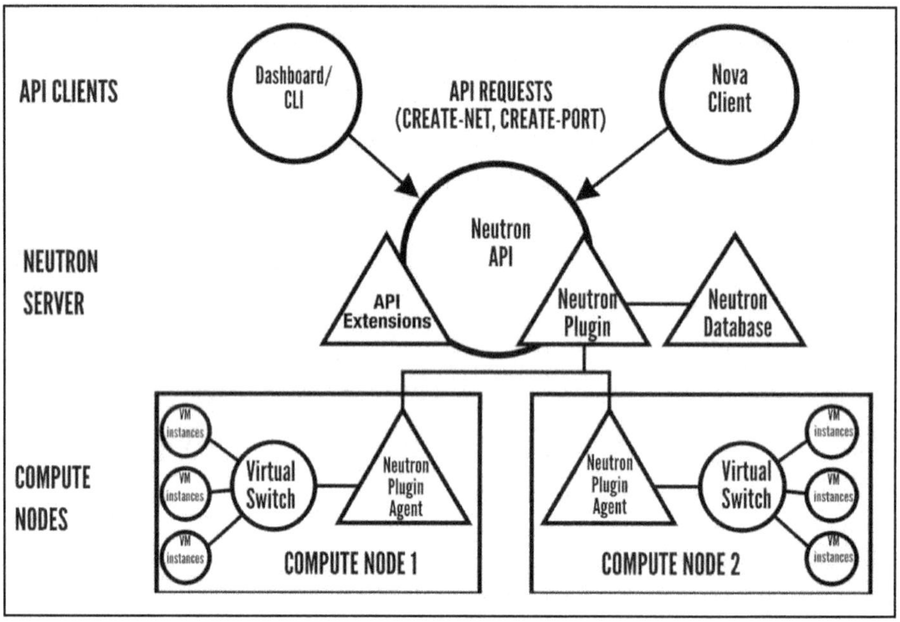

Fig 1.4 Neutron Working

In a cloud environment, neutron provides the tools to achieve this by abstracting the underlying network infrastructure, allowing for complex topologies and advanced networking features, such as:

- Neutron handles both Layer 2 (data link layer) networking, such as VLANs and VXLANs, and Layer 3 (network layer) functions, including routing and NAT.

- Neutron enables administrators to define and apply security policies at the network level through security groups and firewall rules.
- Neutron allows instances to be assigned public IP addresses (floating IPs), enabling external access.
- With VLANs, VXLANs, or GRE tunnels, the Neutron can segment networks to isolate traffic between different tenants or projects.

We now get into installing and configuring the Neutron in our environment:

Install Neutron Packages

At first, we need to verify that the required Neutron and OVN packages are present and that our node has the correct service units available before we apply configuration changes. So here, we will first confirm that the controller has the Neutron server, the ML2 plugin, and the OVN metadata agent, and we will confirm that the OVN central services and Open vSwitch are installed because OVN depends on them.

So, for this, we will run the following checks on the controller node and confirm that the packages are installed and that systemd knows about the relevant units, since our later restart commands depend on these names being available on Ubuntu 24.04.

```
dpkg -l | grep -E "neutron-server|neutron-plugin-ml2|neutron-ovn-metadata-agent|ovn-central|openvswitch-switch"

systemctl list-unit-files | grep -E "neutron|ovn|openvswitch"
```

If any of these above packages are missing, we will correct that by returning to the previous recipe 2 and will align the controller package set.

Configure Neutron Database

Neutron requires a database to store networking information. And for this, we will now create the Neutron database:

```
sudo mysql -u root -p

CREATE DATABASE neutron;

GRANT ALL PRIVILEGES ON neutron.* TO 'neutron'@'localhost' IDENTIFIED BY 'StrongPassword';

GRANT ALL PRIVILEGES ON neutron.* TO 'neutron'@'%' IDENTIFIED BY 'StrongPassword';

FLUSH PRIVILEGES;
```

```
EXIT;
```

Next, we will then synchronize the Neutron schema:

```
sudo neutron-db-manage --config-file /etc/neutron/neutron.conf
--config-file /etc/neutron/plugins/ml2/ml2_conf.ini upgrade
head
```

This step initializes the Neutron database with the required tables for the Flamingo-era Neutron server and ML2 plugin stack.

Configure Neutron

The Neutron configuration involves multiple files. We'll start with the main configuration in **neutron.conf**, located in **/etc/neutron/neutron.conf**. So for this, we will set up the database connection as below:

```
[database]
connection =
mysql+pymysql://neutron:StrongPassword@controller/neutron
```

Next, configure Neutron to authenticate with Keystone:

```
[keystone_authtoken]
auth_uri = http://controller:5000
auth_url = http://controller:5000
memcached_servers = controller:11211
auth_type = password
project_domain_name = Default
user_domain_name = Default
project_name = service
username = neutron
password = StrongPassword
```

The Neutron will use the ML2 plugin for managing Layer 2 networking. So now, we will configure the ML2 plugin in **/etc/neutron/plugins/ml2/ml2_conf.ini**:

```
[ml2]
```

```
type_drivers = flat,vlan,vxlan
tenant_network_types = vxlan
mechanism_drivers = ovn
extension_drivers = port_security
[ml2_type_flat]
flat_networks = provider
[ml2_type_vxlan]
vni_ranges = 1:1000
[securitygroup]
enable_security_group = True
```

This configuration keeps provider networks and VXLAN tenant overlays available, while the OVN backend replaces Linux Bridge entirely.

Configure OVN Integration

We now configure the OVN integration in the **ovn.ini** file. This file binds Neutron to the OVN Northbound and Southbound databases and defines how Neutron advertises itself to OVN.

SO, we now update the following values to match our controller hostnames and the provider network bridge we use for external connectivity.

```
[ovn]
ovn_nb_connection = tcp:controller:6641
ovn_sb_connection = tcp:controller:6642
ovn_l3_scheduler = leastloaded
ovn_metadata_enabled = True
```

The provider mappings are carried by Open vSwitch. We set the bridge mapping so the provider network name aligns with the bridge that attaches to the external network.

Configure DHCP Agent

The OVN provides native DHCP for tenant networks, and our OVN-first deployment does not rely on the Neutron DHCP agent as a primary component. That means , we need to ensure the DHCP agent is not treated as mandatory and to ensure we do not configure Linux Bridge interface drivers. If a DHCP agent unit exists due to older installs, we then need to keep it disabled in our

OVN-first controller setup so it does not conflict with OVN behavior.

```
sudo systemctl disable --now neutron-dhcp-agent 2>/dev/null ||
true
```

This keeps the OVN design consistent and avoids mixing backends.

Configure Metadata Agent

The metadata flow remains important because instances still need to retrieve instance-specific data such as SSH keys and user data. For this, we will now configure the **metadata_agent.ini** so it points at the controller for Nova metadata and so it defines a shared secret that matches the Nova configuration in our **compute** recipe.

```
[DEFAULT]
nova_metadata_host = controller
metadata_proxy_shared_secret = StrongSecret
```

The **metadata_proxy_shared_secret** value must match the corresponding metadata secret in Nova so that metadata requests are trusted end to end.

Configure L3 Agent

The OVN provides distributed logical routing, and our OVN-first deployment does not require the Neutron L3 agent for the default routing behavior. In case, if the service exists due to legacy installs, we will then disable it so the control plane stays purely OVN-backed.

```
sudo systemctl disable --now neutron-l3-agent 2>/dev/null ||
true
```

Register Neutron with Keystone

To allow other OpenStack services to discover and use Neutron, we will register the Neutron service in Keystone's service catalog. We will start by creating the Neutron user, then assign the admin role to that user in the service project. And later, we then create the Neutron service entry, then create the public, internal, and admin endpoints for the Neutron API.

```
openstack user create --domain default --password-prompt
neutron
openstack role add --project service --user neutron admin
openstack service create --name neutron -description
```

```
"OpenStack Networking" network

openstack endpoint create --region RegionOne network public
http://controller:9696

openstack endpoint create --region RegionOne network internal
http://controller:9696

openstack endpoint create --region RegionOne network admin
http://controller:9696
```

These commands register Neutron in the Keystone service catalog, making it available to other OpenStack components.

Start Neutron Services

With the configuration complete, we now start the Neutron services and ensure they are enabled to start automatically on boot.

```
sudo systemctl restart openvswitch-switch ovn-central neutron-
server neutron-ovn-metadata-agent

sudo systemctl enable openvswitch-switch ovn-central neutron-
server neutron-ovn-metadata-agent

openstack network agent list
```

The agent list should show the relevant OVN metadata agent entries as active, and our later network validation will confirm functional connectivity.

Creating Network and Subnet

We will now create a provider network that maps to the provider physical network name we declared in our bridge mappings, then create the provider subnet with the allocation pool and gateway that match our environment.

```
openstack network create --share --provider-network-type flat
--provider-physical-network provider provider

openstack subnet create --network provider --allocation-pool
start=192.168.1.100,end=192.168.1.200 --dns-nameserver 8.8.8.8
--gateway 192.168.1.1 --subnet-range 192.168.1.0/24 provider-
subnet
```

With all these above steps, the Neutron is perfectly ready to manage networks and subnets under an OVN-first architecture.

Recipe 7: Installing and Configuring Nova

Nova is the core compute service within OpenStack, where it manages the lifecycle of VMs or instances. It orchestrates everything from launching instances, managing resources (like CPU, memory, and storage), to handling the shutdown and deletion of instances. The Nova interfaces with other OpenStack services like Glance for retrieving VM images, Neutron for networking, and Cinder for block storage. Its primary function is to provision and manage virtualized compute resources on demand. It supports various hypervisors, including KVM, QEMU, and VMware, offering flexibility in how the compute infrastructure is deployed.

For GitforGits, the deploying and configuring Nova is needed to provide scalable and manageable compute resources.

Installing and Configuring Nova

The Nova consists of several components that need to be installed and configured:

```
sudo apt update
sudo apt install -y nova-api nova-conductor nova-scheduler
nova-novncproxy
```

This command installs the Nova API, conductor, scheduler, and console proxy services.

Configure Nova Database

The Nova also requires a database to store information about instances, flavors, and other compute-related resources. And so, we can do the same creating the Nova and Nova API databases in MySQL:

```
sudo mysql -u root -p
```

Once logged into MySQL, we then create the databases and grant the necessary permissions:

```
CREATE DATABASE nova;
CREATE DATABASE nova_api;
GRANT ALL PRIVILEGES ON nova.* TO 'nova'@'localhost'
IDENTIFIED BY 'StrongPassword';
GRANT ALL PRIVILEGES ON nova.* TO 'nova'@'%' IDENTIFIED BY
'StrongPassword';
GRANT ALL PRIVILEGES ON nova_api.* TO 'nova'@'localhost'
IDENTIFIED BY 'StrongPassword';
```

```
GRANT ALL PRIVILEGES ON nova_api.* TO 'nova'@'%' IDENTIFIED BY
'StrongPassword';

FLUSH PRIVILEGES;

EXIT;
```

Next, we will then synchronize the Nova database schema by running:

```
sudo nova-manage db sync
```

This command initializes the Nova and Nova API databases with the required tables.

Configure Nova

Now, we will configure the Nova service by editing the **nova.conf** file. And this we will do by setting up the database connections:

```
[api_database]

connection =
mysql+pymysql://nova:StrongPassword@controller/nova_api

[database]

connection =
mysql+pymysql://nova:StrongPassword@controller/nova
```

Next, we then configure Nova to authenticate with Keystone:

```
[keystone_authtoken]

auth_uri = http://controller:5000

auth_url = http://controller:5000

memcached_servers = controller:11211

auth_type = password

project_domain_name = Default

user_domain_name = Default

project_name = service

username = nova

password = StrongPassword
```

And then, we will specify the transport URL for messaging between Nova services:

```
[DEFAULT]
transport_url = rabbit://openstack:StrongPassword@controller
```

Finally, we then configure the VNC proxy settings to enable console access to instances:

```
[vnc]
enabled = True
vncserver_listen = $my_ip
vncserver_proxyclient_address = $my_ip
novncproxy_base_url = http://controller:6080/vnc_auto.html
```

Now here, we must replace **`$my_ip`** with the IP address of the controller node and then save and exit the editor.

Configure Nova Compute Service

If we are running a separate compute node, we will need to install and configure the Nova compute service on that node:

```
sudo apt update
sudo apt install -y nova-compute
```

On the compute node, we shall edit the **`nova.conf`** file to point to the appropriate database and messaging service on the controller node:

```
[DEFAULT]
transport_url = rabbit://openstack:StrongPassword@controller
my_ip = 10.0.0.21
[api_database]
connection =
mysql+pymysql://nova:StrongPassword@controller/nova_api
[database]
connection =
mysql+pymysql://nova:StrongPassword@controller/nova
```

Additionally, we will configure the compute node to use the correct hypervisor.

```
[libvirt]
virt_type = kvm
```

After configuring the compute node, we will restart the Nova compute service:

```
sudo systemctl restart nova-compute
```

Register Nova with Keystone

To allow other OpenStack services to discover and use Nova, we will register the Nova service in Keystone's service catalog

```
openstack user create --domain default --password-prompt nova
openstack role add --project service --user nova admin
openstack service create --name nova --description "OpenStack
Compute" compute
```

After this, we will create the public, internal, and admin endpoints for the Nova API:

```
openstack endpoint create --region RegionOne compute public
http://controller:8774/v2.1
openstack endpoint create --region RegionOne compute internal
http://controller:8774/v2.1
openstack endpoint create --region RegionOne compute admin
http://controller:8774/v2.1
```

These above commands register Nova in the Keystone service catalog, and gets it available to other OpenStack components.

Start Nova Services

With the configuration complete, we will now start the Nova services on the controller node and ensure they are enabled to start automatically on boot:

```
sudo systemctl restart nova-api nova-scheduler nova-conductor
nova-novncproxy
sudo systemctl enable nova-api nova-scheduler nova-conductor
nova-novncproxy
```

These commands start the Nova services, which will handle all compute operations within

OpenStack.

Create Flavor

The Flavors define the compute, memory, and storage capacity of instances in OpenStack. To create a standard flavor for GitforGits, simply run the following command:

```
openstack flavor create --id 1 --vcpus 2 --ram 2048 --disk 20
m1.small
```

This creates a flavor named **m1.small** with 2 virtual CPUs, 2 GB of RAM, and 20 GB of disk space.

Launch and Access Instance

Now, we will try to launch a test instance to verify that Nova can deploy virtual machines:

```
openstack server create --flavor m1.small --image CirrOS --nic
net-id=$(openstack network list -f value -c ID) --security-
group default --key-name mykey test-instance
```

This will launch an instance named **test-instance** using the **m1.small** flavor, the CirrOS image, and a key pair named **mykey**.

And, to access the console of the launched instance, we will run the following command:

```
openstack console url show test-instance
```

This command returns a URL that we can open in a web browser to access the instance's console, verifying that the VNC proxy is configured correctly. With this, the Nova is now ready to manage compute resources, launch instances, and scale workloads dynamically based on demand.

Recipe 8: Setting up Cinder for Block Storage

The concept of block storage provides persistent data storage by emulating a physical hard drive. Unlike object storage, which stores data as discrete objects, block storage breaks data into fixed-sized chunks (blocks) and stores them individually. Here, each block has its unique identifier, and the storage system can retrieve blocks independently, making block storage highly efficient for databases, virtual machines, and applications requiring quick access to structured data.

In OpenStack, the block storage is managed by Cinder service. And, the Cinder provides a robust and scalable way to create, attach, and manage block storage volumes that can be used by VMs in Nova. These volumes can be attached to running instances, allowing them to store data persistently even after the instance is terminated. The also Cinder supports a wide range of backend storage solutions, including traditional hard drives, SSDs, and distributed storage systems like Ceph. It also offers advanced features such as snapshots, backups, and volume replication, for maintaining data integrity and availability in enterprise environments.

Cinder Functionalities

Cinder is designed to manage the lifecycle of block storage volumes, providing users with a flexible and reliable way to manage persistent storage. It integrates seamlessly with Nova, and allows instances to attach and use block storage volumes just like physical disks.

The key functionalities of Cinder:

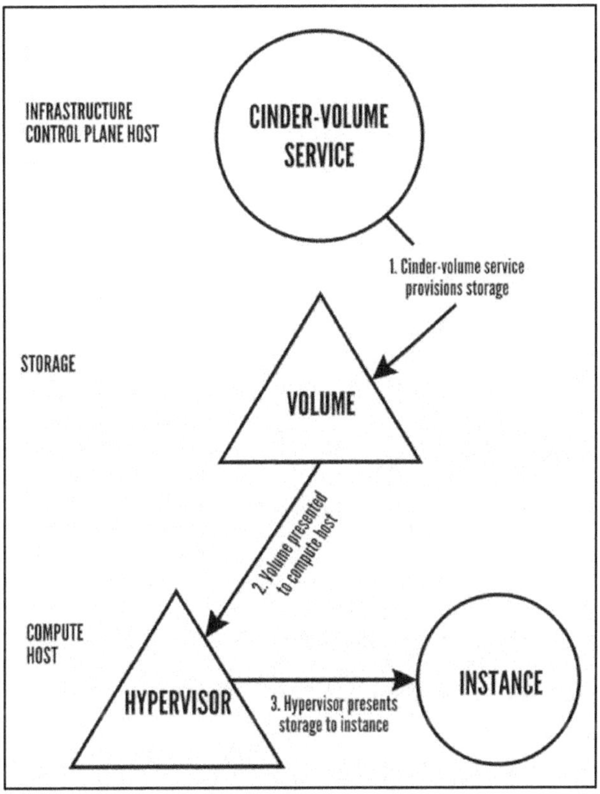

Fig 1.5 Cinder Architecture

- Create, delete, attach, and detach volumes to/from instances.
- Take snapshots of volumes to preserve the state of the data at a particular point in time.
- Create backups of volumes to ensure data safety and recoverability.
- Replicate volumes across different storage backends for high availability and disaster recovery.
- Configure multiple storage backends, such as LVM, Ceph, NFS, or enterprise SANs, to

provide different types of storage.

Configuring Cinder

At first, we will confirm the required services exist and that systemd can manage them.

```
sudo apt update

sudo apt install -y cinder-api cinder-scheduler
```

After this, we move into configuration. Now here, like what we have done so far, the Cinder also requires database to store information about volumes, snapshots, and backups. And for this, we will create Cinder database.

```
sudo mysql -u root -p

CREATE DATABASE cinder;

GRANT ALL PRIVILEGES ON cinder.* TO 'cinder'@'localhost'
IDENTIFIED BY 'StrongPassword';

GRANT ALL PRIVILEGES ON cinder.* TO 'cinder'@'%' IDENTIFIED BY
'StrongPassword';

FLUSH PRIVILEGES;

EXIT;
```

Next, we then synchronize the Cinder database schema:

```
sudo cinder-manage db sync
```

This command initializes the Cinder database with the required tables.

Next, we then configure the Cinder service using **cinder.conf**. To do this, we will first setup the database connection:

```
[database]

connection =
mysql+pymysql://cinder:StrongPassword@controller/cinder
```

We will now configure Cinder to authenticate with Keystone:

```
[keystone_authtoken]

auth_uri = http://controller:5000

auth_url = http://controller:5000
```

```
memcached_servers = controller:11211
auth_type = password
project_domain_name = Default
user_domain_name = Default
project_name = service
username = cinder
password = StrongPassword
```

Here, we need to specify the transport URL for messaging between Cinder services:

```
[DEFAULT]
transport_url = rabbit://openstack:StrongPassword@controller
```

After this, we then need to configure the storage backend. We'll use the default Logical Volume Manager (LVM) backend, and add it to **cinder.conf** file:

```
[lvm]
volume_driver = cinder.volume.drivers.lvm.LVMVolumeDriver
volume_group = cinder-volumes
iscsi_protocol = iscsi
iscsi_helper = tgtadm
[DEFAULT]
enabled_backends = lvm
default_volume_type = lvm
```

Prepare LVM Backend

Since we are using LVM, we need to set up a volume group that Cinder can use to create volumes:

```
sudo pvcreate /dev/sdb
```

Here, we do not forget to replace **/dev/sdb** with the right disk or partition that we intend to use for Cinder volumes. Once done, we just create a volume group named **cinder-volumes**:

```
sudo vgcreate cinder-volumes /dev/sdb
```

This volume group will be used by Cinder to create logical volumes for block storage.

Register Cinder with Keystone

To allow other OpenStack services to discover and use Cinder, we then register the Cinder service in Keystone's service catalog:

```
openstack user create --domain default --password-prompt
cinder
```

And then we assign the **admin** role to the Cinder user in the **service** project:

```
openstack role add --project service --user cinder admin
```

After this, we create the Cinder service entry:

```
openstack service create --name cinder --description
"OpenStack Block Storage" volume

openstack service create --name cinderv2 --description
"OpenStack Block Storage" volumev2

openstack service create --name cinderv3 --description
"OpenStack Block Storage" volumev3
```

And lastly, we create the public, internal, and admin endpoints for the Cinder API:

```
openstack endpoint create --region RegionOne volume public
http://controller:8776/v1/%(tenant_id)s

openstack endpoint create --region RegionOne volume internal
http://controller:8776/v1/%(tenant_id)s

openstack endpoint create --region RegionOne volume admin
http://controller:8776/v1/%(tenant_id)s

openstack endpoint create --region RegionOne volumev2 public
http://controller:8776/v2/%(tenant_id)s

openstack endpoint create --region RegionOne volumev2 internal
http://controller:8776/v2/%(tenant_id)s

openstack endpoint create --region RegionOne volumev2 admin
http://controller:8776/v2/%(tenant_id)s

openstack endpoint create --region RegionOne volumev3 public
http://controller:8776/v3/%(tenant_id)s
```

```
openstack endpoint create --region RegionOne volumev3 internal
http://controller:8776/v3/%(tenant_id)s
openstack endpoint create --region RegionOne volumev3 admin
http://controller:8776/v3/%(tenant_id)s
```

Start Cinder Services

Now with the configuration complete, we can start the Cinder services with enabled auto boot:

```
sudo systemctl enable cinder-scheduler cinder-api
sudo systemctl start cinder-scheduler cinder-api
```

Just to check if Cinder is working correctly:

```
openstack volume list
```

This should return an empty list, indicating that Cinder is operational and ready to manage block storage volumes.

Create, Attach and Access Volume

Now, let us try to create a test volume of 1 GB to verify that Cinder can manage block storage.

```
openstack volume create --size 1 test-volume
```

We then attach it to an existing instance:

```
openstack server add volume test-instance test-volume
```

This attaches the **test-volume** to the **test-instance** launched in the previous recipe. And, to verify that the volume is accessible from the instance, we need to list the available disks:

```
lsblk
```

After this, we should see the **test-volume** listed as an additional disk attached to the instance. We can format and mount the volume within the instance, and can make it available for use.

Recipe 9: Deploying Skyline Dashboard with Keystone Authentication

The Skyline is a modern OpenStack web interface, optimized by UI and UE. It has a modern technology stack and ecology, which is far easy to run and operate with superior concurrency performance.

Technically, it is split into two parts. The first part is **skyline-apiserver**, which handles API-side work and authentication flow, and the other part is **skyline-console**, which provides the browser-facing interface through Nginx. As per the OpenStack documentation, the console expects a ready OpenStack environment with at least Keystone, Glance, Nova, Neutron, and **skyline-apiserver**, which fits exactly where we are in this chapter after bringing up identity, images, compute, networking, and block storage. The Skyline documentation also warns that Horizon and Skyline both default to the same network ports, so we must avoid leaving both on the same listener unless we deliberately rework the port layout. Hence, in our environment, we will use Skyline as the main dashboard entry point for day-to-day operations.

Creating Skyline Database and Keystone User

For Skyline, we need to begin with the API server, because Skyline needs its own database and a service identity in Keystone before the web console can authenticate through it. So, we will create a skyline database, grant access to it, source admin credentials, create a skyline user, and assign the admin role in the service project:

```
sudo mysql -u root -p

CREATE DATABASE skyline DEFAULT CHARACTER SET utf8 DEFAULT
COLLATE utf8_general_ci;

GRANT ALL PRIVILEGES ON skyline.* TO 'skyline'@'localhost'
IDENTIFIED BY 'StrongPassword';

GRANT ALL PRIVILEGES ON skyline.* TO 'skyline'@'%' IDENTIFIED
BY 'StrongPassword';

FLUSH PRIVILEGES;

EXIT;

. admin-openrc

openstack user create --domain default --password-prompt
skyline

openstack role add --project service --user skyline admin
```

This gives Skyline its database and its Keystone-facing service identity, which we were in need before the API server can authenticate and start serving requests.

Configuring 'skyline-apiserver'

We will now deploy the API server. For this, we will clone the repository, install the package, and then we shall create **/etc/skyline** and **/var/log/skyline**. After this, we also need to copy **gunicorn.py** and **skyline.yaml.sample**, changing the Gunicorn bind address to **0.0.0.0:28000**, and then to populate the database.

```
git clone https://opendev.org/openstack/skyline-apiserver.git
sudo python3 -m pip install skyline-apiserver/
sudo mkdir -p /etc/skyline /var/log/skyline
/etc/skyline/policy
sudo cp ${HOME}/skyline-apiserver/etc/gunicorn.py
/etc/skyline/gunicorn.py
sudo sed -i "s/^bind = *.*/bind = ['0.0.0.0:28000']/g"
/etc/skyline/gunicorn.py
sudo cp ${HOME}/skyline-apiserver/etc/skyline.yaml.sample
/etc/skyline/skyline.yaml
cd ${HOME}/skyline-apiserver
make db_sync
```

Next, we will use a configuration block similar to:

```
default:
  database_url:
mysql+pymysql://skyline:StrongPassword@controller:3306/skyline
  log_dir: /var/log/skyline
openstack:
  default_region: RegionOne
  interface_type: public
  keystone_url: http://controller:5000/v3/
  system_project: service
  system_project_domain: Default
  system_user_domain: Default
  system_user_name: skyline
  system_user_password: StrongPassword
  service_mapping:
```

```
    compute: nova
    network: neutron
    block-storage: cinder
    image: glance
    identity: keystone
    placement: placement
```

This step is where the Skyline becomes aligned to our controller endpoints and our Keystone identity flow.

Deploying 'skyline-console'

With the API server configured, we now start it and put the web console in front of it. Here, we launch the Gunicorn, build the console from source, and then exposes it through Nginx with the generated configuration rewritten to point upstream traffic at **0.0.0.0:28000**.

```
sudo tee /etc/systemd/system/skyline-apiserver.service
>/dev/null <<'EOF'

[Unit]

Description=Skyline APIServer

[Service]

Type=simple

ExecStart=/usr/local/bin/gunicorn -c /etc/skyline/gunicorn.py
skyline_apiserver.main:app

LimitNOFILE=32768

[Install]

WantedBy=multi-user.target

EOF

sudo systemctl daemon-reload

sudo systemctl enable skyline-apiserver

sudo systemctl start skyline-apiserver

git clone https://opendev.org/openstack/skyline-console.git
/root/skyline-console

cd /root/skyline-console
```

```
make package
sudo python3 -m pip install --force-reinstall
dist/skyline_console-*.whl
sudo mkdir -p /etc/skyline /var/log/skyline
skyline-nginx-generator -o /etc/nginx/nginx.conf
sudo sed -i "s/server .* fail_timeout=0;/server 0.0.0.0:28000
fail_timeout=0;/g" /etc/nginx/nginx.conf
sudo systemctl enable nginx.service
sudo systemctl start nginx.service
```

At this point, the Skyline API requests flow through Nginx to the API server on port 28000, and the browser-facing console is ready to authenticate through Keystone.

Validating Project Resources

Finally, we validate the Keystone-backed sign-in and visibility of project resources inside the dashboard. For this, we simply sign in with the same Keystone credentials, and move through the compute, network, and storage areas and confirm that the instances we launched, the Neutron networks and subnets we created, and the Cinder volumes we attached are all visible and manageable through the web interface.

```
openstack endpoint list | grep -E
"keystone|nova|neutron|cinder|placement"
systemctl status skyline-apiserver --no-pager
systemctl status nginx --no-pager
ss -lntp | grep -E "80|443|28000"
```

With all these checks complete, the Keystone-backed authentication is in place, the API server is wired to our controller services, the console is fronted by Nginx, and the dashboard surfaces the project resources that matter most to us: instances, volumes, and networks.

Recipe 10: Defining Network Topology for OpenStack Flamingo

In an OpenStack environment, defining a network topology ensures that VMs can communicate with each other, access external networks, and interact with other OpenStack services.

For GitforGits, OVN is the networking backend we use, so Neutron still presents the same API objects, but OVN implements switching, routing, and DHCP behavior through logical constructs backed by Open vSwitch. That means our topology planning remains familiar at the API layer, while the internal dataplane becomes more consistent and scalable in day-to-day operations.

Choosing Network Topology

In the following, we will define four network types and connect them with a router and floating IPs so our cloud supports internal traffic and public access in a structured manner.

Management Network

This network handles internal OpenStack communication between services, such as Neutron, Nova, Cinder, and Keystone. It's needed for the operation of the OpenStack control plane and should be isolated from other networks to enhance security.

Tenant Network

These are the networks created for the instances running in the cloud. Each tenant (or project) can have its own network, which is isolated from other tenants. These networks can be flat, VLAN, or VXLAN-based, depending on the scalability and security requirements.

External (Public) Network

This network allows instances to communicate with the outside world. Instances can be assigned floating IPs from this network to make them accessible from the internet.

Storage Network

This optional network is dedicated to block storage traffic between Cinder and the compute nodes. Separating storage traffic helps in optimizing performance by preventing it from interfering with other network traffic.

Now, let's define and set up this network topology in our OpenStack environment.

Define Management Network

The management network is the backbone of the OpenStack control plane. It should be configured first to ensure that all OpenStack services can communicate effectively.

Create Management Network

```
openstack network create --share --provider-network-type flat
--provider-physical-network provider mgmt-net
```

This command creates a flat network called **mgmt-net** that will be used for internal communication between OpenStack services.

Create Management Subnet

```
openstack subnet create --network mgmt-net --subnet-range
10.0.0.0/24 --gateway 10.0.0.1 --dns-nameserver 8.8.8.8 mgmt-
subnet
```

This creates a subnet on the **mgmt-net** network with the specified IP range. The management network should be isolated from the tenant and external networks to prevent unauthorized access to the control plane.

Define Tenant Network

The tenant network is where the instances will be deployed. This network is isolated from the management network and other tenants' networks. The OVN typically uses an overlay model internally for tenant networks, so our tenant network benefits from consistent east west connectivity without requiring complex physical VLAN allocations per project.

So here, we create the tenant network, create a subnet, and then connect the tenant subnet to a router that will later provide external access through an external gateway.

Given below are the steps:

- We will firstly create the tenant network.

```
openstack network create tenant-net
```

This command creates a network called **tenant-net** that will be used for tenant instances.

- After this, we then create the tenant subnet.

```
openstack subnet create --network tenant-net --subnet-range
192.168.10.0/24 --gateway 192.168.10.1 --dns-nameserver
8.8.8.8 tenant-subnet
```

This creates a subnet on the **tenant-net** network with the specified IP range. Each tenant can have its own network with isolated subnets.

- And finally, we create the router to connect tenant networks to external as following:

```
openstack router create tenant-router

openstack router set tenant-router --external-gateway ext-net

openstack router add subnet tenant-router tenant-subnet
```

This creates a router named **tenant-router**, sets its external gateway to **ext-net** (external network), and connects the tenant subnet to this router. This setup allows instances in the tenant network to access external networks, including the internet.

Define External Network

The external network is where floating IPs are allocated, allowing instances to be accessible from outside the OpenStack environment. The OVN uses the external network as the uplink side of the logical router, and floating IP NAT occurs through the logical router path. We create the external network as an external flat provider network and define its subnet with an allocation pool that provides addresses for floating IP assignments. These addresses must match the reachable public segment in the lab environment, so the IP range in the command is a placeholder that should map to the actual external subnet in our network.

After this step, the Neutron can allocate floating IPs and attach them to instance ports in the tenant network.

To do this:

- We will first create the external network.

```
openstack network create --external --provider-network-type
flat --provider-physical-network provider ext-net
```

This command creates a flat external network named **ext-net**.

- Next, we then create the external subnet.

```
openstack subnet create --network ext-net --subnet-range
203.0.113.0/24 --allocation-pool
start=203.0.113.100,end=203.0.113.200 --dns-nameserver 8.8.8.8
--gateway 203.0.113.1 ext-subnet
```

This creates a subnet on the **ext-net** network with a specific IP range for floating IPs. Instances in the tenant network can be assigned floating IPs from this range to make them accessible from the public internet.

Assign Floating IPs to Instances

Once the networks are set up, we can assign floating IPs to instances to make them accessible from outside the OpenStack environment:

To begin with, we will first Allocate a floating IP:

```
FIP=$(openstack floating ip create -f value -c
floating_ip_address ext-net)
echo $FIP
```

This command allocates a floating IP from the **ext-net** network.

Next, we then associate the floating IP with an instance:

```
openstack server add floating ip test-instance $FIP
```

Replace **test-instance** with the name of the instance and **203.0.113.101** with the floating IP we allocated. This makes the instance accessible from the public network.

Security Groups and Firewall Rules

To secure the network, we must define security groups and firewall rules to control the traffic allowed to and from the instances.

For this, we will first create a security group.

```
openstack security group create web-servers --description
"Security group for web servers"
```

This command creates a security group named **web-servers**.

Next, we then define the ingress rules:

```
openstack security group rule create --protocol tcp --dst-port
22 --remote-ip 0.0.0.0/0 web-servers

openstack security group rule create --protocol tcp --dst-port
80 --remote-ip 0.0.0.0/0 web-servers
```

These commands allow incoming SSH (port 22) and HTTP (port 80) traffic to instances in the **web-servers** security group.

And finally, we then assign the security group to an instance:

```
openstack server add security group test-instance web-servers
```

This assigns the **web-servers** security group to the **test-instance**, ensuring that only allowed traffic can reach the instance.

This above topology includes a management network for internal communication, tenant networks for isolated instance communication, an external network for public access, and an optional storage network for dedicated storage traffic.

Summary

To conclude, we learned to configure OpenStack for GitforGits. First, we configured the hardware and verified that the Linux environment was ready for OpenStack deployment. Next, we discussed how to install and configure Keystone, the identity service required by all OpenStack components to handle authentication and authorization. After that, Glance was configured and installed, making it simple to manage virtual machine images. It was explained in detail how to configure Neutron with the primary goal of creating a robust networking environment capable of handling both internal and external communications in the cloud infrastructure. Nova was then configured to manage computing resources, enabling the creation and management of virtual machine instances. Cinder was created to provide persistent block storage, ensuring that data could be kept secure and easily managed. And finally, the skyline dashboard was established to have better look at instances, resources and networks.

Finally, we designed and implemented a network topology tailored specifically for GitforGits. Each step builds on the previous one, resulting in a fully functional and scalable OpenStack environment.

CHAPTER 2: IDENTITY MANAGEMENT WITH KEYSTONE

Introduction

In this chapter, we will get into the practical aspects and working of Keystone. We previously installed and configured Keystone, hence this chapter will delve deeper into its configuration and management, to fully utilize its capabilities. We will explore how Keystone handles tokens for authenticating and authorizing requests within OpenStack. We will learn to set up RBAC policies for defining who can access specific resources and what actions they can perform. Additionally, we will cover the configuration and use of the Service Catalog towards managing and discovering the various services within the OpenStack environment.

Further, this chapter will teach we how to integrate Keystone with LDAP for centralized user management, implementing multi-domain support for managing multiple organizations or environments within the same OpenStack deployment, and using Keystone Federation to enable authentication across multiple clouds. Finally, we will address common issues that may arise with Keystone and provide troubleshooting strategies to resolve them effectively. By the end of this chapter, we will be able to manage the identity and access within the OpenStack environment for enabling secure and efficient operations.

Recipe 1: Managing Keystone Tokens

The Keystone tokens are essential components in the OpenStack identity service. They are used to authenticate and authorize requests across different OpenStack services. When a user or service requests access to an OpenStack resource, the Keystone issues a token that represents the user's credentials and the permissions they have been granted. This token is then used by the client (user or service) to access OpenStack APIs without having to repeatedly authenticate with username and password.

Exploring Keystone Tokens

There are several types of tokens in Keystone, with **Fernet tokens** being the most used in recent OpenStack deployments due to their security and efficiency. Unlike older token types (such as UUID tokens), the Fernet tokens are lightweight, stateless, and do not require persistent storage, making them ideal for large-scale deployments. These tokens are cryptographically signed and can only be decrypted by Keystone, ensuring that the information they contain remains secure.

Fernet tokens typically have a limited lifespan, after which they expire and must be renewed. This expiration is a key security feature, reducing the risk of token misuse if a token were to be intercepted. Keystone also manages the lifecycle of tokens, including their creation, validation, and revocation. Understanding how to manage these tokens for maintaining the security and efficiency of the OpenStack environment is vital to us.

In the following topics, we will start getting into the practical aspects of managing Keystone tokens, primarily the Fernet tokens.

Viewing Token Information

So, to view details about a specific token, we can use the OpenStack command-line interface (CLI).

```
openstack token issue
```

This command will generate a token and display details such as the token ID, expiration time, and the associated user and project.

Validating Token

To check whether a token is valid (i.e., it has not expired or been revoked), we can use the following command:

```
openstack token show <token_id>
```

If the token is valid, the Keystone will return its details; if it has expired or been revoked, an error message will be displayed.

Revoking Token

In general, the concept of revoking a token invalidates it before its natural expiration, preventing it from being used to access resources. And, this is particularly useful if a security issue is suspected.

So here, to revoke a token:

```
openstack token revoke <token_id>
```

After revocation, any further attempts to use this token will fail most of the time, or rather always.

Managing Fernet Keys

These Fernet tokens rely on a set of cryptographic keys managed by Keystone. These keys are rotated periodically to enhance security. The key repository typically resides in **/etc/keystone/fernet-keys**.

Hence, to manually rotate the keys:

```
sudo keystone-manage fernet_rotate
```

Here, the key rotation ensures that old tokens can be invalidated while maintaining the validity of current tokens. The Keystone manages key rotation automatically, but it's important to understand how to perform this task manually if needed.

Checking Token Expiration Settings

The token expiration settings balance security and usability. And, by default, the tokens have a relatively short lifespan to minimize the window in which a stolen token could be used.

So, to check the current expiration settings, we need to inspect the **keystone.conf**:

```
[token]
expiration = 3600
```

This setting indicates that tokens will expire 3600 seconds (or 1 hour) after they are issued. Adjust this setting as needed based on the security policies.

Auditing and Token Usage

The auditing of token usage can be useful for security and compliance purposes. It helps to track when and how tokens are used within the environment. So, to enable token auditing, we would typically configure logging settings in the **keystone.conf** file.

```
[token]
provider = fernet
expiration = 3600
revocation_cache_time = 3600
audit_log = /var/log/keystone/keystone_token_audit.log
```

This setup tracks token usage and ensures that audit logs are stored for future reference.

Through this recipe, we learned to issue, validate, revoke, and audit tokens, focusing on the use of Fernet tokens for their enhanced security features. In addition, we covered the importance of key rotation and to adjust token expiration settings to suit the security needs.

Recipe 2: Setting up RBAC Policies

The concept of RBAC is quite a fundamental security mechanism in OpenStack to control who can perform specific actions on resources within the cloud environment. The RBAC works by assigning roles to users, and each role defines a set of permissions that determine what actions a user can take. And, these roles are often project-specific, meaning that a user might have different roles in different projects, thus limiting or granting access based on the context.

The RBAC manages access to resources across various departments or teams. For instance, developers might need access to certain compute resources within their project, but not have the ability to modify networking configurations. Conversely, the network administrators might have full control over Neutron services but limited access to compute resources.

In the following, we will learn to setup RBAC policy for GitforGits, and then we will explore how this policy can be applied or limited to specific projects.

Defining Roles

So here, to begin with, we'll create a custom role named **developer** that will have limited access to certain OpenStack services, and another role named **network-admin** with broader access to network-related resources.

```
openstack role create developer
openstack role create network-admin
```

This creates **developer** and **network-admin**. And, both these roles are now available to be assigned to users within specific projects.

Assigning Roles to Users

Once roles are defined, they need to be assigned to users within a project. This assignment determines what each user can do within that project.

For now, we will assign **developer** role to a user named Rohan in a project named **dev-project:**

```
openstack role add --project dev-project --user Rohan
developer
```

This command grants Rohan the **developer** role within the **dev-project**, giving her the permissions associated with that role.

Similarly, we will assign the **network-admin** role to a user named Sara in a project named **network-project**

```
openstack role add --project network-project --user Sara
network-admin
```

After this, the Sara has **network-admin** role within **network-project**, allowing her to manage network resources within that project.

Creating and Applying RBAC Policies

The RBAC policies in OpenStack are generally defined in a policy file, typically located at **/etc/keystone/policy.json** or **/etc/keystone/policy.yaml**. These files define the permissions associated with each role for various OpenStack services.

Editing Policy file

To create custom policies, we would modify the **policy.json** or **policy.yaml** file. For example, to restrict the **developer** role from deleting instances, we might add a policy like this:

```
"compute:delete": "role:admin or role:network-admin"
```

This confirms that only users with the **admin** or **network-admin** roles can delete instances, while those with the **developer** role cannot.

Applying Policy

After editing the policy file, we then restart the Keystone service to apply the changes:

```
sudo systemctl restart keystone
```

The new policies are now in effect, and the users will be limited by the permissions defined in these policies.

Applying RBAC to Specific Projects

The RBAC policies can be applied differently across projects. It allows for fine-grained control over who can do what in each project. For example, let us say that we want the **developer** role to have full access to resources in the **dev-project** but restricted access in another project, say **prod-project**.

So here, we can create different roles or modify the policy to be project-specific. For this, in the **dev-project**, Rohan with the **developer** role, might have permissions to launch instances:

```
"compute:start": "role:developer and
project_id:%(project_id)s"
```

But in the **prod-project**, we might limit this to:

```
"compute:start": "role:developer and project_id:%(project_id)s
and project_name:dev-project"
```

This policy therefore ensures that Rohan can start instances only in the **dev-project** and not in **prod-project**.

Verifying RBAC Implementation

To verify that the RBAC policies are working as expected, we will attempt to perform actions as a user with different roles.

So here, we will test the **developer** role. Here, we will log in as Rohan and try to delete an instance in **dev-project**. The command should fail if the policy is correctly applied:

```
openstack server delete <instance_id>
```

This should return a permission error, confirming that the **developer** role does not have delete permissions.

Similarly, to test the **network-admin** role, we will log in as Sara and try to create a network in **network-project**. The command should succeed, confirming that the **network-admin** role has the necessary permissions:

```
openstack network create test-network
```

If the network is created, we can say that the RBAC policy is working as intended.

Recipe 3: Configuring and Utilizing Service Catalog

In OpenStack, the Service Catalog is a key part of the system, handled by Keystone. It's basically a list of all the services available in the cloud, along with the endpoints connected to them. You can think of it as a central registry, which lets users and other services find and work with OpenStack components. Everything in the catalog is linked to one or more endpoints, which are basically URLs that point to the specific network addresses where the services can be found.

Services and Endpoints

In a service catalog, you usually see three types of endpoints:

- **Public Endpoint** which are accessible from outside the cloud environment. It's usually used by external users or applications that interact with OpenStack services over the internet or a public network.
- **Internal Endpoint** are used for internal communication within the OpenStack environment. It's not exposed to the external world, making it more secure for internal service-to-service interactions. And,
- **Admin Endpoint** are used for administrative tasks and is usually restricted to administrators. It typically offers broader access to manage and configure services.

For our GitforGits project, the internal and admin endpoints secure internal operations and management, while the public endpoint is important for making certain services available to external users or customers.

However, the service catalog should be configured to clearly separate the internal, public, and admin endpoints for secure and efficient access. The internal endpoint will be used for communication between OpenStack services, the admin endpoint for administrative tasks, and the public endpoint for external access where necessary.

So, in the following, we will learn to configure service catalog:

Define Services in Catalog

Before we begin defining, each service in OpenStack must be registered in the service catalog. We can do it by running the following:

```
openstack service create --name nova --description "OpenStack Compute" compute
```

This command registers the Nova service with the type **compute** in the service catalog.

```
openstack service create --name glance --description "OpenStack Image Service" image
```

This registers the Glance service with the type **image**.

```
openstack service create --name neutron --description "OpenStack Networking Service" network
```

This registers the Neutron service with the type **network**.

```
openstack service create --name cinder --description "OpenStack Block Storage" volume
openstack service create --name cinderv2 --description "OpenStack Block Storage v2" volumev2
openstack service create --name cinderv3 --description "OpenStack Block Storage v3" volumev3
```

And, the above command registers the Cinder service with types **volume**, **volumev2**, and **volumev3** for different API versions.

Define Endpoints for Services

After the services are registered, endpoints must be created to make these services accessible. We'll create public, internal, and admin endpoints for each service.

- Endpoints for Nova Service

```
openstack endpoint create --region RegionOne compute public
http://controller:8774/v2.1

openstack endpoint create --region RegionOne compute internal
http://controller:8774/v2.1

openstack endpoint create --region RegionOne compute admin
http://controller:8774/v2.1
```

- Endpoints for Glance Service

```
openstack endpoint create --region RegionOne image public
http://controller:9292

openstack endpoint create --region RegionOne image internal
http://controller:9292

openstack endpoint create --region RegionOne image admin
http://controller:9292
```

- Endpoints for Neutron Service

```
openstack endpoint create --region RegionOne network public
http://controller:9696

openstack endpoint create --region RegionOne network internal
http://controller:9696

openstack endpoint create --region RegionOne network admin
http://controller:9696
```

- Endpoints for Cinder Service

```
openstack endpoint create --region RegionOne volume public
http://controller:8776/v1/%(tenant_id)s

openstack endpoint create --region RegionOne volume internal
http://controller:8776/v1/%(tenant_id)s

openstack endpoint create --region RegionOne volume admin
http://controller:8776/v1/%(tenant_id)s

openstack endpoint create --region RegionOne volumev2 public
http://controller:8776/v2/%(tenant_id)s
```

```
openstack endpoint create --region RegionOne volumev2 internal
http://controller:8776/v2/%(tenant_id)s

openstack endpoint create --region RegionOne volumev2 admin
http://controller:8776/v2/%(tenant_id)s

openstack endpoint create --region RegionOne volumev3 public
http://controller:8776/v3/%(tenant_id)s

openstack endpoint create --region RegionOne volumev3 internal
http://controller:8776/v3/%(tenant_id)s

openstack endpoint create --region RegionOne volumev3 admin
http://controller:8776/v3/%(tenant_id)s
```

Al the above commands create endpoints for all services.

Verifying Service Catalog

Our next step is to verify that all services are correctly registered and that their endpoints are accessible.

So, to see a list of all registered services, use:

```
openstack service list
```

This command displays all the services that have been registered with their names and types.

And, to verify that the endpoints have been created correctly, use:

```
openstack endpoint list
```

This command displays all the endpoints along with their associated services, URLs, and regions.

Testing Endpoint Accessibility

We can also test the accessibility of a specific service endpoint. For example, to test the public endpoint of the Nova service:

```
curl http://controller:8774/v2.1
```

If the service is up and running, we should receive a response, typically an error message related to authentication, indicating that the service is accessible.

This structured approach enhances security and manageability to efficiently operate its cloud infrastructure.

Recipe 4: Integrating Keystone with LDAP

The Lightweight Directory Access Protocol (LDAP) is a protocol used to access and manage directory information over a network. It is widely used for authenticating and authorizing users across various systems, making it a central component in many enterprise environments.

The LDAP integration allows Keystone to authenticate users against an existing directory service, such as Microsoft Active Directory (AD) or OpenLDAP, instead of managing a separate user database. This is particularly beneficial for large organizations that already have an established LDAP infrastructure. It'll streamline identity management and give users a more consistent experience, plus it'll boost security by aligning with the enterprise's existing authentication protocols.

In the following, we will configure Keystone to use LDAP as its backend for identity management.

Configuring LDAP in Keystone

The **`keystone.conf`** needs to be updated to use LDAP as the identity backend. Open the file in a text editor:

```
sudo nano /etc/keystone/keystone.conf
```

In the **`[identity]`** section, we then set the driver to **`ldap`**:

```
[identity]
driver = keystone.identity.backends.ldap.Identity
```

In the **`[ldap]`** section, we will configure the connection details to the LDAP server:

```
[ldap]
url = ldap://ldap.example.com
user = cn=admin,dc=example,dc=com
password = LDAPAdminPassword
suffix = dc=example,dc=com
user_tree_dn = ou=users,dc=example,dc=com
user_objectclass = inetOrgPerson
user_id_attribute = cn
user_name_attribute = cn
user_mail_attribute = mail
```

```
user_enabled_attribute = userAccountControl
user_enabled_mask = 2
user_enabled_default = 512
user_enabled_invert = True
```

In the above, we need to replace **ldap.example.com** with the address of LDAP server, and **LDAPAdminPassword** with the LDAP administrator password. The **suffix** refers to the base DN for the LDAP directory, and **user_tree_dn** points to the subtree where user accounts are stored.

Next, if we want to map LDAP groups to Keystone roles, we can do it by adding the following configuration:

```
role_tree_dn = ou=groups,dc=example,dc=com
role_objectclass = groupOfNames
role_id_attribute = cn
role_name_attribute = cn
role_member_attribute = member
```

This configuration maps LDAP groups located under **ou=groups,dc=example,dc=com** to Keystone roles.

Configuring Keystone for LDAP Backend

After configuring the LDAP connection, we then need to sync the LDAP directory with Keystone to confirm the directory structure is compatible:

```
sudo keystone-manage db_sync
sudo systemctl restart keystone
```

This command updates Keystone's database to reflect the LDAP backend configuration.

Creating LDAP Users and Verifying Integration

After the LDAP is integrated with Keystone, we then create users and assign roles to them directly from the LDAP directory.

So here, we will first create a new user in the LDAP directory. This can be done using an LDAP management tool like **ldapadd** or through an interface provided by the LDAP server (e.g., Active Directory Users and Computers for AD).

After the user is created in LDAP, assign a role to them in Keystone:

```
openstack role add --project dev-project --user
<LDAP_username> developer
```

Here, we will replace **<LDAP_username>** with the username of the LDAP user. This command also assigns the **developer** role to the user within the **dev-project** in OpenStack.

Finally, we then test the LDAP integration by attempting to authenticate with an LDAP user:

```
openstack token issue --os-username <LDAP_username> --os-
password <LDAP_password> --os-auth-url
http://controller:5000/v3 --os-project-name dev-project --os-
user-domain-name Default --os-project-domain-name Default
```

If the configuration is correct, the Keystone will issue a token for the user. Now here, we then need to verify that the user has been assigned the correct roles by listing their roles within the project:

```
openstack role list --project dev-project --user
<LDAP_username>
```

This command should display the roles assigned to the LDAP user within the specified project.

Through this recipe, we configured Keystone to use LDAP as its backend, synchronized the LDAP directory with Keystone, and taught you to create LDAP users and assign roles to them.

Recipe 5: Implementing Multi-Domain Support

The more an organization grows, the more complex its infrastructure becomes. GitforGits might have different departments, teams, or even separate business units, and managing identity and access across a single domain might become limiting and difficult to scale.

That's where multi-domain support in Keystone comes in.

GitforGits' multi-domain support lets you keep users, projects, and roles in different domains separate from each other but still managed together in a single OpenStack deployment. If GitforGits handles sensitive data that needs to be kept separate by law or company rules, multi-domain support makes sure that data stays in the right place, keeping it from getting into the wrong hands. Even as GitforGits grows and adds new teams, departments, or locations, multi-domain support lets the organization expand its identity management without messing with existing setups. You can create new domains for each new business unit or location, so you can grow without messing up the overall structure.

Enabling Multi-Domain Support

To deal with it, we will first open the **keystone.conf** and ensure that the following options are set to enable multi-domain support:

```
[identity]
driver = keystone.identity.backends.sql.Identity
[assignment]
driver = keystone.assignment.backends.sql.Assignment
```

After updating the configuration, we then restart the Keystone service to apply the changes:

```
sudo systemctl restart keystone
```

Creating New Domain

With multi-domain support enabled, we can create new domains to segregate users, projects, and roles.

So here, we will create a new domain for the **Research** department within GitforGits:

```
openstack domain create --description "Research Department
Domain" research-domain
```

This command creates a domain named **research-domain** with a description indicating that it's for the Research department.

Now, to ensure that the domain has been created successfully, we will list all available domains:

```
openstack domain list
```

The output should include **research-domain** along with the default domain.

Creating Domain Users and Projects

After this, we then create users and projects that are specific to the **research-domain**.

Project within New Domain

We will create a project named **research-project** under the **research-domain**:

```
openstack project create --domain research-domain --
description "Project for Research Department" research-project
```

This command creates a project named **research-project** within the **research-domain**.

User within New Domain

We will create a user named **researcher1** within the **research-domain**:

```
openstack user create --domain research-domain --password-
prompt researcher1
```

This command creates a user named **researcher1** and prompts for a password. The user is associated with the **research-domain**.

User Role Assign within Project

And now, we will assign the **member** role to **researcher1** within the **research-project**:

```
openstack role add --project research-project --user
researcher1 member
```

This command assigns the **member** role to **researcher1** for the **research-project** within the **research-domain**.

Managing and Accessing Multiple Domains

With multiple domains in place, now the users must specify their domain when authenticating to ensure they access the correct resources.

User Authentication

So here, to authenticate as **researcher1** in the **research-domain**:

```
openstack token issue --os-username researcher1 --os-password
<password> --os-domain-name research-domain --os-auth-url
http://controller:5000/v3
```

Listing Projects

After authenticating, we can then list the projects accessible to **researcher1**:

```
openstack project list --domain research-domain
```

This command should list the **research-project**, confirming that the user is correctly associated with the domain and project.

Managing Roles across Domains

The multi-domain support also allows for roles to be managed independently across domains. It ensures that permissions can be customized according to the needs of each department.

Creating Custom Role

Let us assume that the Research department requires a special role, **research-admin**, with elevated privileges. So here, we will create the role:

```
openstack role create research-admin
```

This role can now be assigned to users within the **research-domain** as needed.

Assign Custom Role

We can then assign the **research-admin** role to a user within the **research-domain**:

```
openstack role add --project research-project --user
researcher1 research-admin
```

This command assigns the **research-admin** role to **researcher1** within the **research-project**.

Through this recipe, we enabled multi-domain support, created a new domain, set up users and projects within that domain, and explored how to manage roles across domains.

Recipe 6: Using Keystone Federation for Multi-Cloud Authentication

There is something called as Keystone Federation. It is a powerful feature that enables identity sharing across multiple OpenStack clouds or between OpenStack and other identity providers. Essentially, it allows users to authenticate in one cloud (or identity provider) and gain access to resources in another cloud without needing separate credentials for each environment.

The federation relies on establishing trust relationships between different identity providers and service providers. In a federated setup, the Keystone acts as the service provider, while an external identity provider (which could be another Keystone instance or a completely different system like an enterprise SSO) handles user authentication. Once authenticated, the user's identity is asserted across the different clouds or environments.

Why Multi-Cloud Authentication?

For a growing organization which might leverage different cloud environments for various purposes, such as public clouds for scalable workloads, private clouds for sensitive data, or even different OpenStack clouds for regional operations, the management of these multiple identities and credentials is a challenge and quite cumbersome. So here, the multi-cloud authentication is something that simplifies it.

It allows:

- Users to authenticate using their primary credentials and access resources across multiple clouds.
- The federation to confirm that sensitive credentials are not spread across multiple clouds. Instead, the authentication is handled by a trusted identity provider, and only temporary, scoped access tokens are shared between environments.
- To streamline the access across clouds so that the teams can efficiently move workloads or data between environments without facing authentication barriers.

In the following, we will learn to configure the Keystone Federation to enable multi-cloud authentication in the OpenStack environment.

Setting up Identity Provider (IdP)

To learn this, we will assume that GitforGits has two OpenStack environment. One is a primary environment (acting as IdP) and the other is a secondary environment (acting as the Service Provider).

Configure IdP

On the IdP, we will configure Keystone to act as the IdP. For this, we will edit the **keystone.conf**:

```
[federation]
remote_id_attribute = HTTP_OIDC_ISS
```

This will set up the attribute that will be used to identify users authenticated via federation.

Create IdP in Keystone

After this, we will then register the IdP with Keystone:

```
openstack identity provider create --remote-id
http://idp.example.com idp
```

In the above, we need to replace the **http://idp.example.com** with the actual URL of the IdP.

Create Mapping for IdP

The Mappings define how incoming federated assertions (user attributes) are translated into local Keystone user identities.

So here, we will create the mapping for IdP:

```
openstack mapping create --rules '[
{
    "local": [
        {
            "user": {
                "name": "{0}",
                "domain": {
                    "name": "Default"
                }
            }
        },
        {
            "group": {
                "name": "federated_users",
                "domain": {
                    "name": "Default"
                }
            }
        }
    ],
    "remote": [
        {
            "type": "openstack_user"
        }
    ]
```

```
}
]' idp_mapping
```

This mapping associates federated users with a local domain and user group in Keystone.

Associate Mapping with IdP

Next, we then associate the **idp_mapping** with IdP:

```
openstack identity provider set --mapping idp_mapping idp
```

This completes the setup on the IdP side.

Setting up Service Provider (SP)

The next step is to configure the secondary OpenStack environment to act as a SP that will trust the IdP.

Register SP in IdP

On the IdP environment, we will create a SP entry that represents the SP:

```
openstack service provider create --auth-url
https://sp.example.com/v3/OS-
FEDERATION/identity_providers/idp/protocols/saml2/auth --
service-provider-url
https://sp.example.com/Shibboleth.sso/SAML2/POST sp
```

Here, we will replace **https://sp.example.com** with the actual URL of the SP. It tells IdP to communicate with the SP.

Configure SP

On the SP environment, we can configure Keystone to recognize and trust the IdP. Here, we will edit **keystone.conf** on the SP:

```
[federation]
trusted_dashboard = https://sp.example.com/dashboard
[auth]
methods = external,password,token,oauth1,saml2
```

This configuration ensures that the SP accepts authentication from the IdP.

Create Protocol for SP

On the SP, we then register the protocol (e.g., SAML2) used for federated authentication:

```
openstack federation protocol create --identity-provider idp -
-mapping idp_mapping saml2
```

This links the **saml2** protocol with the IdP and the mapping that was created earlier.

Federating Users across Clouds

Now that the IdP and SP are set up, the users can authenticate with the IdP and access resources in the SP.

Create Federated Roles

On both the IdP and SP, we will create roles that will be used for federated users. For example, we can create a role named **federated_user**:

```
openstack role create federated_user
```

This role will be assigned to federated users to grant them specific permissions.

Assign Federated Roles to Users

And finally, we will assign the **federated_user** role to a user in the SP:

```
openstack role add --user <user_name> --project <project_name>
federated_user
```

here, we just need to replace the **<user_name>** and **<project_name>** with the actual user and project names. It will allow the federated user to access the project resources in the SP environment.

This setup is particularly valuable in multi-cloud scenarios, where the organization leverages various cloud environments for different purposes. Through this recipe, we configured Keystone to act as both an IdP and a SP, established trust relationships between these environments, and demonstrated how users can authenticate and access resources across clouds using federated identity.

Recipe 7: Troubleshooting Keystone Failures

While implementing Keystone, we might run into few challenges and errors. And it could be configuration mistakes, service integration problems, authentication failures, or federation related.

In the following, we'll examine the root cause of the issues and will teach you the practical troubleshooting tips, and hacks to get them resolved.

Service Start Failure

One of the most common issues is the Keystone service fails to start after initial configuration or after changes have been made. Now, this can be due to incorrect configuration files, missing dependencies, or problems with the underlying database.

Check Configuration files

So here, the first step is to check the **keystone.conf** for any syntax errors or incorrect settings. We can refer to tools like **cat** or **less** to inspect the file and ensure that all settings are correctly configured.

```
cat /etc/keystone/keystone.conf
```

Verify Database Connection

If you do not know, but the Keystone relies heavily on its database. Hence, it is necessary the database settings in the **[database]** section of **keystone.conf** are correct, and that the database is accessible.

We can easily test the connection to the database using a command like:

```
mysql -u keystone -p -h controller
```

If the database connection fails, then we need to check the credentials and network accessibility between Keystone and the database server.

Inspect Logs

The Keystone logs are also quite useful for diagnosing issues. The logs are in **/var/log/keystone/keystone.log.** We can anytime assess the logs for any error messages or stack traces or why the service failed to start.

```
tail -f /var/log/keystone/keystone.log
```

After making changes, we simply need to restart the Keystone service and monitor the logs to see if the issue persists:

Authentication Failure

At times, the users are unable to authenticate with Keystone. And, it results in errors like "Invalid user/password" or "Could not find token."

Validate Credentials

So here, we need to ensure the user credentials (username, password, domain, and project) are correct:

```
openstack token issue --os-username <username> --os-password
<password> --os-project-name <project_name> --os-auth-url
http://controller:5000/v3
```

If the token is issued successfully, then we can say that the credentials are correct.

Check Keystone Logs

The authentication issues are often logged in the Keystone logs. So, we simply do as we did earlier to inspect the logs:

```
grep -i "authentication" /var/log/keystone/keystone.log
```

Verify User and Role Configuration

Here, we need to ensure if the user is correctly assigned to the appropriate roles and projects. To see, we will go to OpenStack CLI where we can list the roles and verify the user assignments:

```
openstack role list --user <username> --project <project_name>
```

Check Token Expiry

If tokens are being issued but authentication fails later, then we need to check the token expiration settings in the **`keystone.conf`** file. The tokens that expire too quickly might cause unexpected authentication failures as well.

```
[token]
expiration = 3600  # 1 hour
```

So here, we need to consider extending the token expiration time if that is the cause.

Token Validation Issue

Sometime, the Keystone fails to validate tokens, and it often results in errors like "Token not found" or "Invalid token."

Proper Token Management

If we are using Fernet tokens, then we must see if the key repository is properly managed. The key files are in **/etc/keystone/fernet-keys/** and we must ensure if they are intact and have the correct permissions.

```
ls -l /etc/keystone/fernet-keys/
```

Rotate Fernet Keys

If the token validation issues persist, then we must consider rotating the Fernet keys. This can help resolve issues related to corrupted keys or synchronization problems between Keystone nodes.

```
sudo keystone-manage fernet_rotate
```

After rotation, we shall confirm if the key distribution mechanism (e.g., rsync) is correctly synchronizing the keys across all Keystone nodes.

Check Token Cache

And, if we are using a caching mechanism like Memcached, then we must check if the cache is functioning properly. Because, the issues with the token cache can cause validation failures. So here, we need to restart Memcached to clear any stale cache entries:

```
sudo systemctl restart memcached
```

Federation Configuration Issue

The federation setup between IdPs and SPs sometimes fail, and it leads to issues like "Federated authentication not working" or "Cannot find federated user."

Verify IdP and SP Configuration

So here, we need to ensure that both the IdP and SP are correctly configured which includes setting up the federation mappings and protocols in Keystone.

```
openstack federation protocol list --identity-provider <idp>
```

Check SAML Assertions

If we are using SAML2 for federation, then we need to inspect the SAML assertions being exchanged between the IdP and SP. For this, we can use a tool like **SAML Tracer** to capture and analyze the SAML assertions.

Sync Time between IdP and SP

The time synchronization is a key in a federated setup. For this, we need to check if both the IdP and SP have their clocks synchronized using NTP. If the clocks are out of sync, then the token validation might fail.

```
sudo systemctl restart ntp
```

Inspect Apache and Keystone Logs

In addition, the federated authentication involves Apache for handling SAML2, so here we need to inspect both, the Apache logs and the Keystone logs for errors related to federation.

```
tail -f /var/log/apache2/error.log
```

LDAP Integration Issue

The Keystone also can fail to authenticate users against an LDAP directory. And, it may lead to errors like "LDAP connection failed" or "User not found in LDAP."

Verify LDAP Connectivity

So here, the first step is to check that the Keystone can connect to the LDAP server. We can use tools like **ldapsearch** to test the connection and query the LDAP directory from the Keystone node.

```
ldapsearch -x -H ldap://ldap.example.com -D
"cn=admin,dc=example,dc=com" -W -b
"ou=users,dc=example,dc=com"
```

If the connection fails, then we need to check the network connectivity, LDAP server status, and credentials.

Check LDAP Configuration

The next is to review the LDAP settings in the **keystone.conf**. Here, we nees to check if the **url**, **user**, **password**, **user_tree_dn**, and other relevant fields are correctly configured.

```
[ldap]

url = ldap://ldap.example.com

user = cn=admin,dc=example,dc=com

password = LDAPAdminPassword

user_tree_dn = ou=users,dc=example,dc=com
```

Inspect Keystone Logs

In the Keystone logs, we need to look for LDAP-specific errors in the logs:

```
grep -i "ldap" /var/log/keystone/keystone.log
```

Proper SSL/TLS Configuration

If we are using LDAPS (LDAP over SSL), then we shall check if the SSL/TLS is correctly configured and that the Keystone node trusts the LDAP server's certificate. If needed, then we need to update the **keystone.conf** with correct certificate paths.

```
[ldap]
use_tls = True
tls_cacertfile = /etc/ssl/certs/ca-certificates.crt
```

RBAC Issue

Regarding RBAC, there are users who are unable to perform actions which ideally, they are permitted to do. And these leads to errors like "Unauthorized action" or "Access denied."

Verify Role Assignments

So, for this, we need to confirm if the user has been assigned the correct roles within the appropriate project or domain:

```
openstack role assignment list --user <username> --project
<project_name>
```

Check Policy Files

The Keystone uses policy files to enforce RBAC. So here, we need to confirm if the **policy.json** or **policy.yaml** file is correctly configured, and that the permissions for the roles are as intended.

```
cat /etc/keystone/policy.json
```

Refresh Policy Cache

If you've made changes to the policy file, then we might need to clear Keystone's policy cache to apply the changes:

```
sudo keystone-manage token_flush
```

```
sudo systemctl restart keystone
```

Use Debug Mode

We can also enable the debug mode in the **`keystone.conf`** file to get more detailed logging information, which can help in diagnosing RBAC issues:

```
[DEFAULT]
debug = True
```

After enabling debug mode, we just need to restart the Keystone and then we can review the logs for detailed error messages.

Service Catalog Issue

Sometime, the services fail to appear in the service catalog, or the endpoints are not accessible. And, it then leads to errors like "Service not found" or "Endpoint unreachable."

Check Service and Endpoint Registration

So here, we can begin with checking if the services and their endpoints are correctly registered in the service catalog:

```
openstack service list
openstack endpoint list
```

And then we need to verify if the endpoints have the correct URLs and are associated with the correct regions.

Test Endpoint Accessibility

Here, we can make use of **`curl`** to test the accessibility of service endpoints directly:

```
curl http://controller:8774/v2.1  # For Nova API
```

If the endpoint is not accessible, then we can check the service configuration and network settings.

Inspect Keystone Logs for Service Catalog Errors

We can also investigate the Keystone logs:

```
grep -i "service catalog" /var/log/keystone/keystone.log
```

Overall, we've explored and tried to resolve the Keystone issues, right from the service startup failures to authentication problems, token validation issues, federation configuration challenges, LDAP integration, RBAC issues, and service catalog errors.

Summary

To summarize, we have almost mastered the concept of identity management within OpenStack using Keystone service. It started with Keystone tokens, including issuing, validating, revoking, and rotating tokens, for maintaining secure and efficient authentication processes. Next, the concept of RBAC was introduced, where roles were created and assigned to users within specific projects, ensuring that access to resources was appropriately controlled. The chapter then covered the configuration and use of the Service Catalog, emphasizing how to register services and define endpoints to ensure proper service discovery and access.

Later, we learned the integration of Keystone with LDAP for centralized user management. We also implemented the multi-domain support in managing separate organizational units within the same OpenStack deployment. Finally, we explored the Keystone Federation for multi-cloud authentication wherein we explored the trust between different clouds or IdPs. The chapter finally concluded with troubleshooting Keystone issues.

CHAPTER 3: IMAGE MANAGEMENT WITH GLANCE

Introduction

Glance is the service that stores, discovers, and retrieves virtual machine images in OpenStack. In this chapter, we will explore this aspect of image management. Previously, we focused on setting up the OpenStack infrastructure and managing identity via Keystone, and now in this chapter, we will learn to efficiently manage images for deploying instances across cloud environment. We will learn to create and register images in Glance, ensuring that the appropriate templates are available for the virtual machines. We will also learn to create custom images using cloud-init, which allows for the automated configuration of instances at launch.

Later, we will go over managing the metadata and properties. We learn to configure Glance for various storage backends, such as Swift and Ceph, to optimize image storage and access. It will also teach to automate image uploads using Glance CLI. It covers showing how to manage image versions and updates such that the instances always use the most current and secure images. And lastly, in this chapter, we will learn to secure and encrypt images in Glance for staying compliant with security standards.

Recipe 1: Creating and Registering Images

Glance is the OpenStack Image Service. It provides services for discovering, registering, and retrieving virtual machine images. These images serve as templates from which instances are created. Efficient image management ensures the availability of right configurations and operating systems for deployment across the cloud environment.

In this recipe, we will learn to create and register images in Glance. And, before we can create and register images, we will also get the Glance CLI installed and configured.

Installing Glance CLI

The Glance CLI is part of the OpenStack client package. It is a powerful tool to interact with the Glance service directly from the command line.

Now, if we have already installed the OpenStack client on the system, then Glance CLI is available. However, if not, then we can install it by first updating the package list:

```
sudo apt update
```

Next, we then install the OpenStack client, which includes the Glance CLI:

```
sudo apt install -y python3-openstackclient
```

Now, to verify that the Glance CLI is installed, we run the check at the version of the OpenStack client:

```
openstack --version
```

Here, we should see a version number output, so we can affirm that the client is installed.

After this, we need to source the OpenStack RC file. This file contains environment variables that define how the CLI interacts with the OpenStack environment.

So, we will source the RC file using:

```
source ~/openstack.rc
```

Here, we have to replace the **`~/openstack.rc`** with the actual path to the RC file. This step ensures that the CLI commands are authenticated and directed to the correct OpenStack environment.

Creating Image

After this, we can now create and register images in Glance.

Build Image

Firstly, we need an image file that we can upload to Glance. This could be a pre-built image such as an Ubuntu Cloud image or a custom-built image that you've prepared. For our project, we'll use a CirrOS image:

```
wget http://download.cirros-cloud.net/0.5.2/cirros-0.5.2-
x86_64-disk.img
```

Create Image

Next, we then use the Glance CLI to create an image entry in Glance:

```
openstack image create "CirrOS" --disk-format qcow2 --
container-format bare --file cirros-0.5.2-x86_64-disk.img --
public
```

Now here in the above code,

- **`"CirrOS"`** is the name of the image.
- **`--disk-format qcow2`** is the format of the image file.
- **`--container-format bare`** specifies that the image is not within another container format.
- **`--file cirros-0.5.2-x86_64-disk.img`** is the path to the image file. And,

- **--public** makes the image public so that any project can use it.

Verify Image Creation

After the image is created, we run a quick verify:

```
openstack image list
```

It should display the CirrOS image along with its ID, status, and other details.

Registering Image

In some cases, we might have an image stored in a different location or need to re-register an existing image. So here, we do it as shown below:

Registering External Image

If we have an image stored externally, then we can register it without uploading it directly:

```
openstack image create "External Image" --disk-format qcow2 --
container-format bare --location
http://example.com/images/external-image.qcow2 --public
```

Here, the **--location** specifies the URL where the image is stored. The Glance will reference this URL when the image is needed.

Updating Image Metadata

If we need to update the metadata of an existing image (such as its visibility or format), then we can do so using:

```
openstack image set --property key=value --public <image_id>
```

In the above, we just need to replace **<image_id>** with the ID of the image we want to update. It will then modify the properties and access control of the image.

Deleting Image

If we need to remove an image from Glance, we can also do that easily using:

```
openstack image delete <image_id>
```

This will remove the image from the Glance repository.

With these above skills, we can ensure that the necessary virtual machine templates are readily available for deployment across their OpenStack environment.

Recipe 2: Building Custom Images using 'cloud-Init'

The **cloud-Init** is a widely used tool for initializing cloud instances. It is responsible for performing the initial configuration of a cloud instance when it first boots, such as setting up SSH keys, configuring the hostname, installing packages, and running user-defined scripts. cloud-init is supported by most Linux distributions and cloud platforms, including OpenStack.

In this recipe, we will learn cloud-init, and build and register custom images.

Installing 'cloud-init'

Most modern Linux distributions come with cloud-init pre-installed. However, if we are working with a base image that doesn't include cloud-init, then we need to install it manually:

```
sudo apt update
sudo apt install -y cloud-init
```

Once installed, the cloud-init automatically runs on the first boot of the instance. I have also outlined below a simple example of a cloud-init configuration that updates the package list and installs Apache:

```
#cloud-config
package_update: true
packages:
  - apache2
runcmd:
  - echo "Hello, World!" > /var/www/html/index.html
```

This configuration tells cloud-init to update the package list, install Apache, and create a simple web page.

Building Custom Image with 'cloud-init'

We now proceed to build a custom image.

Prepare Base Image

So here, we will begin with a base image which we are aiming to customize. We can use an existing Ubuntu image, or we can download one:

```
wget http://cloud-images.ubuntu.com/focal/current/focal-server-cloudimg-amd64.img
```

Customize Image

We will use a tool like **virt-customize** from **libguestfs** suite to inject files into the image:

```
sudo apt install -y libguestfs-tools
sudo virt-customize -a focal-server-cloudimg-amd64.img --run-command 'cloud-init clean'
sudo virt-customize -a focal-server-cloudimg-amd64.img --copy-in cloud-init-config.yaml:/etc/cloud/cloud.cfg.d/
```

Here, the **cloud-init-config.yaml** is the custom cloud-init configuration file, which is copied into the **/etc/cloud/cloud.cfg.d/** directory within the image.

Verify 'cloud-init' Configuration

After injecting the configuration, we will verify it by mounting the image and inspecting the files:

```
sudo guestmount -a focal-server-cloudimg-amd64.img -i /mnt
cat /mnt/etc/cloud/cloud.cfg.d/cloud-init-config.yaml
sudo guestunmount /mnt
```

This will validate that the configuration has been correctly applied to the image.

Upload Custom Image to Glance

Now once the custom image is ready, the next step is to upload it to Glance so that it can be used to launch instances in OpenStack.

```
openstack image create "Custom-Ubuntu-CloudInit" --file focal-server-cloudimg-amd64.img --disk-format qcow2 --container-format bare --public
```

This command uploads the customized image to Glance and makes it available for use in the OpenStack environment.

Launch Instance using Custom Image

And then finally, we will launch a new instance using the custom image to see cloud-init in action:

```
openstack server create --flavor m1.small --image Custom-Ubuntu-CloudInit --network private --key-name mykey custom-instance
```

Once the instance is launched, we will SSH into it and verify that the cloud-init configuration has been applied:

```
ssh -i mykey.pem ubuntu@<instance_ip>
```

After this, we should see "Hello, World!" message on the default web page. Now, to streamline the process of building and uploading custom images with cloud-init, we can automate it using a bash script:

```
#!/bin/bash

# Variables

IMAGE_NAME="Custom-Ubuntu-CloudInit"

BASE_IMAGE="focal-server-cloudimg-amd64.img"

CLOUD_INIT_CONFIG="cloud-init-config.yaml"

# Download the base image

wget http://cloud-images.ubuntu.com/focal/current/$BASE_IMAGE

# Install libguestfs-tools if not already installed

sudo apt install -y libguestfs-tools

# Inject cloud-init config into the image

sudo virt-customize -a $BASE_IMAGE --run-command 'cloud-init clean'

sudo virt-customize -a $BASE_IMAGE --copy-in $CLOUD_INIT_CONFIG:/etc/cloud/cloud.cfg.d/

# Upload the image to Glance

openstack image create "$IMAGE_NAME" --file $BASE_IMAGE --disk-format qcow2 --container-format bare --public

# Launch an instance from the custom image (optional)

# openstack server create --flavor m1.small --image $IMAGE_NAME --network private --key-name mykey custom-instance
```

This above script automates the downloading of the base image, customizing it with cloud-init, and uploading it to Glance. Overall, in this recipe, we learned using cloud-init to build custom images in Glance.

Recipe 3: Managing Image Metadata and Properties

Glance also helps in managing images that serve as templates for launching virtual machines. Now, these images are not just raw data files, as they come with associated metadata and properties that describe various aspects, such as format, architecture, size, and specific configurations.

This recipe will explore various tasks associated with managing image metadata and properties in Glance. We'll learn to view, add, update, and delete metadata properties for images, as well as how to use these properties to enhance image management.

Image Metadata and Properties Overview

What Are Metadata and Properties?

The metadata refers to a set of data that describes and gives information about other data, in this case, the image. Metadata can include information such as the image name, size, checksum, disk format, and more.

And, the properties are specific attributes associated with an image, which can be custom-defined to suit specific use cases. These properties might include details such as operating system type, architecture, image version, and custom tags.

Why Manage Metadata and Properties?

Taking care of image metadata and properties gives us the ability:

- To organize and categorize images by assigning them meaningful properties based on their purpose or configuration.
- To pick the right image when launching instances. It ensures we are using the best image.
- To quickly search and find the images we're looking for, that fit specific criteria.
- To enforce policies, like we can make sure that only images with certain security configurations are used in production environments.

Viewing Image Metadata and Properties

Before managing image properties, we need to learn to view the existing metadata and properties associated with an image.

List All Images

The following command will list all images along with their basic metadata:

```
openstack image list
```

It displays a table with columns such as ID, Name, Status, and Visibility. While this provides a quick overview, it doesn't show detailed properties.

View Detailed Metadata and Properties

To view detailed metadata and properties of a specific image, we can use **openstack image show** followed by image ID or name:

```
openstack image show <image_id>
```

This then provides a comprehensive list of metadata and properties, including the disk format, container format, size, checksum, and any custom properties.

Adding Image Metadata and Properties

After viewing the metadata, we might want to add new properties or update existing ones to better manage the images.

Add Custom Properties to Image

The custom properties can be added to an image to provide additional information that is not covered by the default metadata. For example, we might want to tag an image with the operating system version or designate it as a "golden" image.

So here, if we want to add a custom property, we can then use **openstack image set**:

```
openstack image set --property os_version="Ubuntu 20.04" --
property image_type="golden" cirros
```

In the above, two properties are added to the image named **cirros**:

- **os_version** is set to "Ubuntu 20.04".
- **image_type** is set to "golden".

Update Properties

If we need to update an existing property, we can use the same **openstack image set** with the new value for the property:

```
openstack image set --property os_version="Ubuntu 22.04"
<image_id_or_name>
```

This command updates the **os_version** property of the specified image to "Ubuntu 22.04".

Verify Properties

After adding or updating properties, we can also verify that the changes have been applied correctly:

```
openstack image show <image_id_or_name>
```

This will display the updated list of properties, including any new or modified ones.

Deleting Image Properties

In some cases, we might need to remove a property from an image, especially if it's no longer relevant or was added by mistake.

Delete Specific Property

To delete a specific property from an image, we can use the **--property** flag with the **openstack image unset**:

```
openstack image unset --property image_type cirros
```

This removes the **image_type** property from the **cirros** image.

Verify Property Deletion

After deleting a property, we can verify its removal using **openstack image show**:

```
openstack image show <image_id_or_name>
```

After this, the output should no longer include the deleted property.

Image Metadata for Enhanced Management

The image metadata can be leveraged to enhance image management, particularly in large-scale OpenStack environments where many images are in use.

Organizing Images by Tags

The tags are a powerful way to categorize images. We can add tags to images using the **openstack image set**:

```
openstack image set --tag "production" cirros
```

This thing tags the **cirros** image with "production".

Searching Tagged Images

We can search for images by tags, making it easy to retrieve all images that belong to a specific category:

```
openstack image list --tag "production"
```

It then lists all images tagged with "production".

Implementing Image-based Policies

We can also enforce policies based on image properties. For example, we can restrict certain operations (like launching instances) to images that meet specific criteria by filtering the images based on properties:

```
openstack server create --image <image_id_or_name> --flavor
<flavor> --network <network> <server_name>
```

Automating Metadata Management

For environments with many images, we can automate the management of image metadata and properties to save significant time and reduce errors.

Automate Metadata Tasks

So here, we can use the bash scripts to automate the addition, updating, or removal of image properties. Given below is a simple script to tag all images of a specific operating system:

```
#!/bin/bash
OS_VERSION="Ubuntu 20.04"
TAG="ubuntu-20.04"
images=$(openstack image list --property
os_version=$OS_VERSION -f value -c ID)
for image in $images; do
    openstack image set --tag $TAG $image
done
```

This script tags all images with the **os_version** property set to "Ubuntu 20.04" with the tag "ubuntu-20.04".

Automated Reporting on Image Metadata

We can then generate reports on image metadata to monitor and review the properties of all images in the environment with the following script:

```
openstack image list -f json > images.json
jq '.[] | {ID: .ID, Name: .Name, Properties: .Properties}'
images.json > image_report.json
```

This script generates a JSON report of all images and their properties to review and manage image metadata.

With good management of metadata, we can improve how images are organized, found, and used in the OpenStack environment. And whether it's tagging images for easy categorization or using properties to enforce policies, managing metadata is key to maintaining a well-organized and efficient cloud infrastructure. With automation and best practices, we can make sure that image management stays scalable, consistent, and in line with your company's goals.

Recipe 4: Configuring Glance for Different Backends (Swift, Ceph)

Introduction to Object Storage Systems

When managing images in OpenStack, the choice of storage backend for Glance is vital for performance, scalability, and reliability. The Glance supports various storage backends, with OpenStack Swift and Ceph being two of the most popular options. And, each backend offers unique advantages which is suitable for different use cases.

Swift Object Storage

The OpenStack Swift is an object storage system designed to store and retrieve large amounts of unstructured data at scale. The Swift is particularly well-suited for cloud environments that require high availability and fault tolerance. It achieves this by distributing data across multiple nodes and replicating it to ensure durability. Its architecture is designed for scalability, and hence it is an excellent choice for environments that expect significant growth in storage needs.

Ceph Object Storage

And, the Ceph is a distributed storage system that provides object, block, and file storage in a unified platform. Unlike Swift, the Ceph offers a more versatile solution with its ability to handle different types of data. It is highly regarded for its performance, scalability, and resilience, and thus it is ideal for environments that require a high level of data redundancy and performance, especially when dealing with block storage for virtual machines and object storage for large datasets.

Knowing our GitforGits' requirements, the Ceph is likely the better choice considering the unified storage, better scalability and comparatively better data redundancy.

Configuring Glance for Ceph

Now that we've decided to use Ceph as the backend storage for Glance, we'll configure the Glance accordingly.

Prepare Ceph Cluster

At first, we will see to getting the Ceph cluster properly set up and running. If Ceph is not yet installed, we will need to install and configure it first. For this recipe, we assume that Ceph is already installed and functional.

Create Ceph Pool

The Glance requires a dedicated pool in Ceph where images will be stored. So here, we will create a new pool named **images**:

```
ceph osd pool create images 128 128
```

It thus creates a pool named **images** with 128 placement groups. We can adjust the number of placement groups based on the cluster size and requirements.

Create Client Keyring

The Glance also needs access to the Ceph cluster via a client keyring. So here, we will create a client key for Glance:

```
ceph auth get-or-create client.glance mon 'allow r' osd 'allow
class-read object_prefix rbd_children, allow rwx pool=images'
```

This creates a new keyring entry for the **client.glance** user, granting it read and write access to the **images** pool.

After this, we just save the keyring to a file:

```
ceph auth get-or-create client.glance >
/etc/ceph/ceph.client.glance.keyring
```

While saving, we need to ensure that the keyring file is accessible by the Glance service.

Configuring Ceph on Glance Node

Install Ceph Client Packages

On the node where Glance is running, we need to install the Ceph client packages:

```
sudo apt update
sudo apt install -y ceph ceph-common
```

It thus allows Glance to communicate with the Ceph cluster.

Configure Ceph

After this, we then need to copy the **ceph.conf** from a Ceph node:

```
scp user@ceph-node:/etc/ceph/ceph.conf /etc/ceph/
```

While copying, just replace the **user@ceph-node** with the appropriate user and Ceph node hostname. And then verify that the configuration is correct by listing the Ceph pools:

```
ceph osd lspools
```

After this, we should be able to see the **images** pool listed.

Configuring Glance for Ceph Use

Now that the Ceph client is configured on the Glance node, it's time to configure Glance to use Ceph as its backend.

So here, we will first open the **glance-api.conf** and update **[DEFAULT]** and **[glance_store]** sections to use Ceph.

```
[DEFAULT]
# Other existing configurations...
show_image_direct_url = True
[glance_store]
stores = rbd,file,http
default_store = rbd
rbd_store_pool = images
```

```
rbd_store_user = glance
rbd_store_ceph_conf = /etc/ceph/ceph.conf
rbd_store_chunk_size = 8
rbd_store_image_format = 2
```

In the above code, you may notice the following key configuration options:

- **stores** lists the available storage backends. Here, **rbd** (RADOS Block Device, used by Ceph) is listed.
- **default_store** specifies **rbd** as the default storage backend for Glance.
- **rbd_store_pool** specifies the Ceph pool where images will be stored.
- **rbd_store_user** specifies the Ceph client user (**glance**). And,
- **rbd_store_ceph_conf** points to the Ceph configuration file.

After this, we shall confirm the **glance** user on the Glance node has appropriate permissions to access the Ceph keyring:

```
sudo chown glance:glance /etc/ceph/ceph.client.glance.keyring
sudo chmod 600 /etc/ceph/ceph.client.glance.keyring
```

After this, we then restart the Glance API service to apply the changes:

```
sudo systemctl restart glance-api
```

Monitoring Ceph Backend

Monitor Ceph Health

It's also important to regularly check on the health of the Ceph cluster. If Glance can always access the image data, it'll work fine.

```
ceph status
```

It simply provides an overview of the Ceph cluster's health, including any warnings or errors.

Expanding Storage

As the image repository grows, we may need to expand the Ceph storage pool. We can add more OSDs (Object Storage Daemons) to the Ceph cluster to increase capacity and performance:

```
ceph osd create
```

you may refer to the official Ceph documentation, in case if you are looking to add and configure new OSDs.

Basically, we looked into setting up Glance to use Ceph as the storage backend for GitforGits. With Ceph as the backend, we can get a solid and scalable storage solution that makes sure images are stored safely and can be retrieved quickly for instance deployment.

Recipe 5: Automating Image Uploads using Glance CLI

In dynamic cloud environments, frequent updates to virtual machine images are quite common and a routine practice too. It may include new security patches, application configurations, or entirely new OS versions. If we consider manually uploading and managing these images, it can become time-consuming and error-prone.

So, in this recipe, we will learn automating the process of uploading images to Glance. We will create a script that can be scheduled to run at regular intervals or triggered by specific events, like the availability of a new image version.

Creating Automation Script

Before we begin automating the image upload process, we need to confirm if the Glance CLI is installed. If not, you just need to refer to the previous recipe to get it installed. Apart from this, the OpenStack RC file containing the environment variables must be sourced too, to allow our script interact with the Glance.

If all is in place as said above, then you can create or refer to the following automation script **auto_upload_image.sh**:

```
#!/bin/bash
# Define variables
IMAGE_NAME="Custom-Ubuntu-CloudInit"
IMAGE_FILE="/path/to/image.img"
DISK_FORMAT="qcow2"
CONTAINER_FORMAT="bare"
IMAGE_VERSION="v1.2"  # Optional versioning
# Source the OpenStack RC file
```

```
source ~/openstack.rc
# Check if the image already exists
existing_image=$(openstack image list --name $IMAGE_NAME -f
value -c ID)
if [ -n "$existing_image" ]; then
    echo "Image '$IMAGE_NAME' already exists with ID:
$existing_image"
    # Check if the existing image should be replaced (e.g.,
based on version or other criteria)
    existing_version=$(openstack image show $existing_image -f
value -c properties | grep "version")
    if [ "$existing_version" == "$IMAGE_VERSION" ]; then
        echo "The existing image is already at version
$IMAGE_VERSION. No need to upload."
        exit 0
    else
        echo "Updating the image to version $IMAGE_VERSION..."
        openstack image delete $existing_image
    fi
fi
# Upload the new image
echo "Uploading new image '$IMAGE_NAME'..."
openstack image create "$IMAGE_NAME" \
    --file $IMAGE_FILE \
    --disk-format $DISK_FORMAT \
    --container-format $CONTAINER_FORMAT \
    --property version="$IMAGE_VERSION" \
    --public
# Verify the upload
uploaded_image=$(openstack image list --name $IMAGE_NAME -f
value -c ID)
```

```
if [ -n "$uploaded_image" ]; then
    echo "Image '$IMAGE_NAME' successfully uploaded with ID:
$uploaded_image"
else
    echo "Image upload failed."
    exit 1
fi
```

In the above script:

- **IMAGE_NAME** specifies the name of the image to be uploaded.
- **IMAGE_FILE** points to the location of the image file.
- **DISK_FORMAT** and **CONTAINER_FORMAT** define the format of the image.
- **IMAGE_VERSION** is an optional variable that can be used to track the version of the image.

The **source ~/openstack.rc** command checks for the necessary environment variables to interact with OpenStack. The script also uses **openstack image list** to check if an image with the specified name already exists. If the image exists, then the script checks if the version matches the version defined in the script. If the versions match, then the script exits without uploading a new image. Otherwise, the existing image is deleted to make way for the new version.

Later, the script uses **openstack image create** to upload the image. It sets the image name, file path, disk format, container format, and any additional properties such as version. The **--public** flag makes the image available to all projects. And after uploading, the script verifies that the image was successfully added to Glance by checking the image list again.

Script Scheduling using Cron

To fully automate the image upload process, we can schedule the script to run at regular intervals using cron. This could be to check for new image versions daily and upload them if available.

So, to do this, we open the crontab for the current user:

```
crontab -e
```

Then, we add a new cron job to run the script every day at 2 AM:

```
0 2 * * * /path/to/auto_upload_image.sh >>
/var/log/auto_upload_image.log 2>&1
```

It schedules the script to run daily at 2 AM and log the output to **auto_upload_image.log**. This script can be extended to handle more complex scenarios like, if we need to upload multiple images, we can improvise the script to loop through a list of images:

```
declare -A IMAGES=(
    ["Ubuntu-20.04"]="/path/to/ubuntu-20.04.img"
    ["CentOS-8"]="/path/to/centos-8.img"
)
for IMAGE_NAME in "${!IMAGES[@]}"; do
    IMAGE_FILE="${IMAGES[$IMAGE_NAME]}"
    # Repeat the upload process for each image
    # ...
done
```

It then manages and automates the upload of multiple images in a single script.

Custom Metadata and Tags

We can also add custom metadata and tags during the image upload process by extending the **openstack image create** with additional **--property** and **--tag** options as shown below:

```
openstack image create "$IMAGE_NAME" \
    --file $IMAGE_FILE \
    --disk-format $DISK_FORMAT \
    --container-format $CONTAINER_FORMAT \
    --property version="$IMAGE_VERSION" \
    --property os_version="Ubuntu 20.04" \
    --tag "production" \
    --public
```

If the images are stored in a remote repository, we can extend the script to fetch the latest image before uploading it:

```
wget -N http://repository.example.com/images/latest.img -O
/path/to/image.img
```

Here, the **-N** option ensures that the image is only downloaded if it's newer than the local copy. We can also configure the script to send notifications or alerts if an image upload fails. For example, we can use **mail** or **sendmail** to send an email if the script encounters an error:

```
if [ -z "$uploaded_image" ]; then
    echo "Image upload failed." | mail -s "Image Upload 
Failure" admin@example.com
    exit 1
fi
```

Overall, this whole process drives us to streamline the management of images successfully. It gives us confirmation about the latest versions being always available in Glance.

Recipe 6: Managing Image Versions and Updates

In any cloud environment, managing different versions of virtual machine images is critical to maintaining consistency, security, and stability. With updates getting released to operating systems, applications, and configurations, we are needed to confirm that the cloud infrastructure is running the correct version of each image.

So, in this recipe, we will manage image versions and updates to efficiently track, update, and maintain image versions across the environment.

Tagging Image Versions

The first step is to establish a versioning strategy. It could involve using semantic versioning (e.g., 1.0, 1.1, 2.0) or any another system that is preferred by most of the developers in the team.

Creating New Image Version

Whenever we create a new version of an image, we must tag it with a version number to distinguish it from previous versions. For example, if we have an image named **Ubuntu-20.04** and we want to create a new version **1.1**, we would do the following:

```
openstack image create "Ubuntu-20.04-v1.1" \
    --file /path/to/ubuntu-20.04-v1.1.img \
    --disk-format qcow2 \
    --container-format bare \
```

```
    --property version="1.1" \
    --property os_version="Ubuntu 20.04" \
    --public
```

It uploads the new image version and tags it with the **version** property, which is then easy to identify.

Tagging Images

The tags are another way to manage image versions. For example, we can tag an image as **latest** to indicate that it is the most current version:

```
openstack image set --tag latest Ubuntu-20.04-v1.1
```

If we later upload a new version, we can remove the **latest** tag from the old version and apply it to the new one:

```
openstack image unset --tag latest Ubuntu-20.04-v1.1
openstack image set --tag latest Ubuntu-20.04-v1.2
```

This will allow us to quickly identify and deploy the latest image version.

Viewing Image Versions

Now here, if we want to view all versions of a particular image:

```
openstack image list --property os_version="Ubuntu 20.04"
```

This lists all images with the specified operating system version to see the available versions.

Updating Images

When you update images in Glance, you're basically replacing older versions with newer ones. That way, you can be sure that all instances are using the latest updates. This is especially important when it comes to applying security patches or making configuration changes.

Uploading Updated Image

When a new version of an image becomes available, we simply need to upload it to Glance with an incremented version number:

```
openstack image create "Ubuntu-20.04-v1.2" \
    --file /path/to/ubuntu-20.04-v1.2.img \
```

```
    --disk-format qcow2 \
    --container-format bare \
    --property version="1.2" \
    --property os_version="Ubuntu 20.04" \
    --public
```

This will upload the updated image and tags it with the new version number.

Deprecating Older Versions

Similarly, we can deprecate the older versions by setting a custom property or removing the **`public`** visibility:

```
openstack image set --property deprecated=true Ubuntu-20.04-v1.0
```

Alternatively, we can also make the older image private, so it's no longer visible to all users:

```
openstack image set --private Ubuntu-20.04-v1.0
```

Replacing Instances with Updated Images

With a new image version made available, we need to update existing instances. So here, we need to create a new instance from the updated image and then migrate data from the old instance in following steps:

We first create a new instance using the updated image:

```
openstack server create --flavor m1.small --image Ubuntu-20.04-v1.2 --network private --key-name mykey updated-instance
```

Next, we then use tools like **`rsync`** or **`scp`** to migrate data from the old instance to the new one.

Once the migration is complete, we then delete the old instance:

```
openstack server delete old-instance
```

Doing like this, the applications are always running on the latest and the most secure image versions.

Version Rollback

Sometimes, after deploying a new image version, we may discover issues. And such issues demand us to roll back to a previous version.

So here, we will first list the available versions of an image to identify the version to which we need to roll back:

```
openstack image list --property os_version="Ubuntu 20.04"
```

We will find the version number or image name we wish to revert to.

And then, we will use the previous image version to launch a new instance:

```
openstack server create --flavor m1.small --image Ubuntu-20.04-v1.0 --network private --key-name mykey rollback-instance
```

If we use tags to manage versions, then we revert the **`latest`** tag to the previous version to ensure that new instances are launched with the rollback image:

```
openstack image unset --tag latest Ubuntu-20.04-v1.2

openstack image set --tag latest Ubuntu-20.04-v1.0
```

Automating Image Version Management

We can extend the automation to image version management too. We can automate the image upload process with the following script:

```
#!/bin/bash

IMAGE_NAME="Ubuntu-20.04"

NEW_VERSION="v1.3"

IMAGE_FILE="/path/to/ubuntu-20.04-v1.3.img"

existing_image=$(openstack image list --name $IMAGE_NAME-$NEW_VERSION -f value -c ID)

if [ -z "$existing_image" ]; then

    echo "Uploading new image version $NEW_VERSION..."

    openstack image create "$IMAGE_NAME-$NEW_VERSION" \

        --file $IMAGE_FILE \

        --disk-format qcow2 \

        --container-format bare \
```

```
        --property version="$NEW_VERSION" \
        --property os_version="Ubuntu 20.04" \
        --public
else
    echo "Image version $NEW_VERSION already exists."
fi
```

This script checks if a specific image version exists and uploads it if it does not.

In addition, we can extend the script to manage tags, such that the latest image version is always tagged correctly:

```
# Remove the latest tag from the old version
openstack image unset --tag latest Ubuntu-20.04-v1.2
# Set the latest tag on the new version
openstack image set --tag latest Ubuntu-20.04-v1.3
```

After this, we can also schedule the script to run automatically:

```
crontab -e
0 2 * * * /path/to/upload_image_version.sh >>
/var/log/upload_image_version.log 2>&1
```

This ensures that new image versions are consistently uploaded and managed without manual intervention.

Overall, we covered creating and tagging new image versions, updating images, rolling back to previous versions when necessary, and automating the management process.

Recipe 7: Securing and Encrypting Images

In cloud environments, images are critical assets, knowing that they contain the operating systems, applications, and configurations, which are necessary to run virtual machines. However, these images can also pose to be a significant security vulnerability too. Things like unauthorized access to images can be a fatal issue. In several high-profile data breaches, attackers have gained access to unencrypted images, allowing them to extract sensitive information, such as passwords, private keys, and configuration files.

Sometimes, the attackers attempt to inject malware or backdoors into images stored in the cloud, which then unknowingly gets deployed across multiple instances, leading to widespread system compromise and data exfiltration. A significant number of cloud environments still store images in plaintext, which also makes them vulnerable to interception and unauthorized access, particularly in multi-tenant environments where images are shared across different users and projects. Also, the Internal actors having access to the cloud infrastructure can also misuse their privileges to access, modify, or delete images.

Hence, it is quite a recommended activity or a feature which must be practiced while operating an Openstack environment. In the following recipe, we will learn to secure and encrypt images to mitigate all such risks.

Secure Access Controls

The first step in securing images is to enforce strict access controls within Glance to limit who can view, modify, or delete images.

Restricting Image Visibility

By default, images in Glance can be marked as public, private, or shared. To limit access to only authorized users or projects, images should be set to private or shared with specific projects only:

```
openstack image set --private <image_id>
```

This ensures that only the project that owns the image can view or use it.

Assigning Image Roles

We then implement RBAC to further restrict who can manage images. Here, we assign specific roles that allow only certain users to upload, modify, or delete images:

```
openstack role add --user <user_name> --project <project_name>
image-admin
```

This role could be limited to administrators or trusted users, ensuring that image management is tightly controlled.

Audit and Monitoring

After this, we enable auditing and monitoring of image-related activities. For this, we will configure the Glance to log all actions performed on images, including creation, deletion, and access attempts:

```
sudo nano /etc/glance/glance-api.conf
```

In it, we then enable the following settings:

```
[DEFAULT]
debug = True
[oslo_middleware]
audit = True
audit_map_file = /etc/glance/api_audit_map.conf
```

After making these changes, we will restart the Glance API service:

```
sudo systemctl restart glance-api
```

Encrypting Images

The concept of encrypting images almost guarantees us that even if an unauthorized party gains access to the image files, they cannot read or tamper with the contents without the decryption key.

So here, if Glance is already configured to use Ceph as the backend which we have already done in the previous chapter, then we can leverage Ceph's native encryption capabilities to encrypt images at rest.

We just need to enable encryption on a per-pool basis or for specific images:

```
rbd create --size <size> --image-feature layering,encryption -
-image <image_name>
```

This command will then create a new encrypted RBD image. Once we have it, we can then upload it to Glance:

```
openstack image create "Encrypted-Image" --file
/path/to/encrypted_image.img --disk-format qcow2 --container-
format bare --public
```

The image remains encrypted while stored in Ceph. It is protected even if an attacker gains access to the storage backend.

We can also encrypt images before uploading them to Glance so that they remain secure even during transfer. For this, we can use OpenSSL to encrypt the image file before uploading it:

```
openssl enc -aes-256-cbc -salt -in /path/to/image.img -out
/path/to/encrypted_image.img -k <password>
```

And then, we upload the encrypted image to Glance:

```
openstack image create "Encrypted-Image" --file
/path/to/encrypted_image.img --disk-format qcow2 --container-
format bare --public
```

When we need to use the encrypted image, we simply download it and decrypt it using OpenSSL:

```
openssl enc -aes-256-cbc -d -in /path/to/encrypted_image.img -
out /path/to/decrypted_image.img -k <password>
```

Secure Storage and Provisioning

There is a service called as OpenStack Barbican. It is designed for secure storage, provisioning, and management of secrets, like the encryption keys and passwords. If we integrate Barbican with Glance, then we can pursue automated and secure key management for image encryption as shown below:

We will primarily get it installed and configured:

```
sudo apt install barbican-api barbican-keystone-listener
barbican-worker
```

After this, we then configure Barbican to work with Glance. For this, we simply update the **glance-api.conf**:

```
[barbican]

auth_endpoint = http://<barbican_endpoint>:9311
```

in the above, we replace **<barbican_endpoint>** with the actual Barbican service endpoint.

After this, we then create an encryption key in Barbican:

```
openstack secret store --name "glance-image-key" --payload-
content-type "application/octet-stream" --payload-content-
encoding "base64" --payload <base64-encoded-key>
```

next, we then use the stored key to encrypt the image and upload it to Glance:

```
openstack image create "Barbican-Encrypted-Image" --file
/path/to/image.img --disk-format qcow2 --container-format bare
--property "encryption-key"="<key_id>" --public
```

Now, when we launch the instance from encrypted image, the Glance automatically retrieves the key from Barbican.

Secure Image Distribution

In addition to encrypting images at rest and during upload, it's needed to secure the distribution of images across the network, particularly in multi-tenant environments or when images are shared between different regions.

Secure Image Transfer

At first, we will confirm that all communications between Glance and other OpenStack services, such as Nova and Cinder, are encrypted using SSL/TLS. This will prevent unauthorized interception or tampering with image data during transfer.

Enable SSL/TLS

After this, we then edit the Glance configuration file **`glance-api.conf`** to enable SSL/TLS:

```
[DEFAULT]
use_ssl = True
cert_file = /etc/ssl/certs/glance.crt
key_file = /etc/ssl/private/glance.key
```

And then, we will restart the Glance service to apply the changes:

```
sudo systemctl restart glance-api
```

Overall, in this recipe, we explored the critical aspects of securing and encrypting images in OpenStack's Glance service. Additionally, we covered secure image distribution and the importance of ongoing monitoring and maintenance to ensure the integrity and security of images in the cloud environment.

Summary

To summarize, we have certainly mastered around image management using Glance. We used Glance CLI to upload and manage images efficiently. We then created custom images using cloud-init. The management of image metadata and properties was also covered, with a focus on adding, updating, and utilizing metadata to organize and optimize image usage. We configured Glance to use various storage backends, especially Ceph.

Later, we experimented with automating image uploads. We learned managing image versions and updates, including different versions of images, updating existing images, and revert to earlier versions. The chapter finally concluded with image encryption, wherein it detailed each step to use encryption and secure access controls to protect images in the cloud.

Chapter 4: Networking with Neutron

Introduction

So far in this book, we've covered Keystone identity management, and Glance image management. With Neutron at its heart, this chapter will move our attention to OpenStack's networking capabilities, specifically to manage connections to internal networks.

In this chapter, we will learn how OpenStack networking will operate when Neutron is built on an OVN-first foundation. We will begin by understanding the network types that matter in a practical cloud environment, including provider-style connectivity and tenant-side isolation. After that, we will configure the Neutron plugin model and the OVN backend so that logical switching, logical routing, metadata flow, and security enforcement work together as one consistent networking layer. This will give us a clear operational model for how traffic will move inside the GitforGits environment and how Neutron objects will be translated into real network behavior by OVN.

As we continue through the chapter, we will move into hands-on network deployment by creating provider networks, tenant networks, subnets, routers, and floating IP paths. We will validate both east-west and north-south traffic so that we do not stop at configuration alone. We will also build Layer 2 segments through VLAN-backed networks and Geneve-based overlay networks so that we can understand where physical mapping ends and logical tenant isolation begins. Toward the end of the chapter, we will work with OVN operationally by using OVN CLI tools to inspect logical switches, routers, ports, chassis information, and backend state. By the time we complete the chapter, we will have learned not only how to create Neutron networks, but also how to verify, operate, and troubleshoot OVN-backed OpenStack networking in a practical cloud setting.

Recipe 1: Understanding OpenStack Network Types

Neutron provides connectivity as a service between interface devices managed by other OpenStack services. It supports a variety of network types that cater to different use cases and deployment scenarios. Our networking backend is OVN, so the Neutron API objects stay familiar, while the implementation for switching, routing, DHCP, and security groups is delivered through OVN logical constructs backed by Open vSwitch. This means we still think in networks, subnets, routers, and ports, but the "how it is implemented on the dataplane" becomes more consistent and easier to operate once we adopt OVN as the default mechanism driver.

In this recipe, we walk through the network types Neutron supports, including flat and VLAN for provider style connectivity, and an overlay network type for tenant segmentation at scale. Our networking backend is OVN, so the Neutron API objects stay familiar, while the implementation for switching, routing, DHCP, and security groups is delivered through OVN logical constructs backed by Open vSwitch. This means we still think in networks, subnets, routers, and ports, but the "how it is implemented on the dataplane" becomes more consistent and easier to operate once we adopt OVN as the default mechanism driver.

Exploring Neutron Network Types

Flat Network

A flat network is a simple network type where all instances share a single network, and there is no network segmentation. All instances are on the same broadcast domain. Flat networks are typically used in small-scale environments or for management networks where segregation is not required. Since there is no segmentation, flat networks are not suitable for multi-tenant environments or scenarios where security isolation is a priority.

In our OVN-first setup, a flat provider network still has value because it maps cleanly to a physical uplink through an Open vSwitch bridge mapping, and it works well for an external network that provides floating IPs or for a shared network segment that represents control plane reachability.

VLAN (Virtual LAN)

VLAN is a network segmentation method that uses the IEEE 802.1Q standard to tag traffic on different virtual networks over a single physical network. Each VLAN has its own unique identifier (VLAN ID). VLANs are ideal for multi-tenant environments where network isolation between tenants is necessary. They provide a secure way to segregate traffic while sharing the same physical infrastructure. VLANs are limited by the number of available VLAN IDs (up to 4096), which can be a constraint in large-scale environments.

In an OVN-first design, VLAN provider networks remain a practical option for north-south traffic patterns, while tenant networks typically use an overlay so that tenant growth does not force continuous allocation of physical VLAN IDs.

Geneve (Overlay network for tenant segmentation with OVN)

The OVN commonly uses an overlay encapsulation to connect tenant networks across compute nodes without requiring physical VLAN segmentation per tenant. Geneve is the encapsulation method that is typically used with OVN for tenant overlay networking. Conceptually, this fills the same role that VXLAN filled in many earlier Neutron designs, because it allows many isolated tenant segments to be created without exhausting VLAN IDs. The Neutron API still expresses tenant networks through standard constructs, but the implementation relies on OVN logical switching and routing, and the tunnel traffic is carried over the underlay network between hypervisors.

The practical takeaway is that, we keep flat and VLAN for provider networks where the physical network matters, and we rely on Geneve overlay for tenant networks to scale segmentation cleanly.

VXLAN (Virtual Extensible LAN)

VXLAN is an overlay network technology that extends the VLAN ID space by encapsulating Layer 2 frames within UDP packets, allowing for network segmentation at a much larger scale. VXLAN can support a very large number of segments, and it has been a common overlay choice in Neutron designs that use Open vSwitch agents.

In an OVN-first architecture, VXLAN becomes less central because OVN's tenant overlay commonly uses Geneve. VXLAN can still appear in some environments due to existing tooling or older operational expectations, so understanding the concept remains useful. The main operational difference is that our configuration and troubleshooting focus stays on OVN databases, OVN logical topology, and Open vSwitch integration, rather than on an Open vSwitch agent that creates VXLAN tunnels on behalf of Neutron.

GRE (Generic Routing Encapsulation)

The GRE is another tunneling protocol used to encapsulate network traffic, like VXLAN. GRE creates point-to-point links that can tunnel traffic across different networks. GRE is used in scenarios where simple tunneling is required without the need for the additional features provided by VXLAN. It's often used in conjunction with VPNs. GRE lacks the scalability and flexibility of VXLAN and is generally used in more specific, less complex network setups.

GitforGits currently operates a network topology that includes segmented networks for different departments, such as development, testing, and production. The organization requires secure network isolation between these segments while allowing for scalability as the company grows. The network infrastructure uses a mix of VLANs and flat networks, with a focus on simplicity and ease of management.

GitforGits currently operates a network topology that includes segmented networks for different departments, such as development, testing, and production. The organization requires isolation between these segments while allowing for scalability as the company grows. The network infrastructure uses a mix of VLANs and flat networks, with a focus on simplicity and ease of management. Given Neutron's capabilities and the needs of GitforGits, VLAN works well for provider networks that map to physical segmentation. A tenant overlay is a better long-term fit for project networks that must scale beyond physical VLAN allocation. OVN provides that overlay model through logical networking, so we can keep our provider mapping stable and allow tenant networks to scale without continuous physical VLAN work.

Configuring Neutron

Given GitforGits' requirements and the existing infrastructure, VLAN is a suitable choice for provider segments. To future-proof the environment and allow for greater scalability, a tenant overlay is the appropriate long-term solution. Our OVN-first approach means we do not use the Open vSwitch agent model that the first edition of this book used. Instead, we configure the ML2 plugin to use the OVN mechanism driver and we configure the Geneve overlay range for tenant networks.

We will first edit the Neutron configuration **`ml2_conf.ini`** to enable OVN with Geneve:

```
[ml2]
type_drivers = flat,vlan,geneve
tenant_network_types = geneve
mechanism_drivers = ovn
extension_drivers = port_security
[ml2_type_geneve]
vni_ranges = 1000:5000
max_header_size = 38
```

This configuration sets Geneve as the tenant overlay type and defines a range of tunnel identifiers.

After this, we will restart Neutron services, so that the OVN-first mechanism driver and Geneve settings take effect:

```
sudo systemctl restart neutron-server neutron-ovn-metadata-agent
```

Next, we will then create a test network and we then view network details to confirm the tenant network type aligns with our configuration:

```
openstack network create test-tenant-network
openstack network list --long
```

This recipe walked through the network types supported by Neutron and aligned those types to an OVN-first approach where provider networks use flat or VLAN and tenant networks use an overlay through Geneve. We also aligned GitforGits topology needs to that model so isolation and scalability are achieved without continuous physical segmentation work.

Recipe 2: Configuring Neutron Plugins and Agents with OVN

In Neutron, plugins and agents enable and manage network services. The plugins are responsible for managing L2 and L3 networking, security groups, and DHCP, while the agents are responsible for implementing these services on the physical or virtual network infrastructure.

There are different types of plugins and agents in Neutron. The most commonly used plugin remains the Modular Layer 2 (ML2) plugin because it supports multiple network types and allows different mechanisms to be selected. Our mechanism choice is OVN. This changes the "agent story" compared to an Open vSwitch agent or Linux Bridge agent design. The OVN central services run on the controller, OVN chassis runs on each node that participates in networking, and Neutron interacts with OVN through OVN databases. The Neutron still exposes the same API to users and to Nova, but the implementation responsibilities are shifted into OVN's logical networking model rather than into multiple Neutron agents.

For GitforGits, our target is a network architecture that supports provider network connectivity, tenant isolation, floating IPs, and metadata access for instances. The ML2 plugin remains the control plane entry point, and OVN becomes the mechanism driver that implements L2 and L3 behaviors. The DHCP is delivered by OVN for tenant networks, routing is delivered by OVN logical routers, and security group enforcement is delivered through OVN integration with Open vSwitch.

Neutron Plugins and Agents Overview

ML2 Plugin

The ML2 plugin supports a variety of L2 network types, and it is modular, allowing different mechanisms to be used. In this configuration, ML2 is paired with the OVN mechanism driver. This allows Neutron to continue offering flat and VLAN for provider networks and an overlay for tenant networks, while OVN implements logical switching and logical routing. This keeps our configuration aligned with scalability needs and reduces the number of moving parts that must run as separate Neutron agents.

L3 Plugin

L3 routing behavior remains a key requirement because floating IPs and external access depend on routing and NAT. With OVN, L3 behavior is implemented through OVN logical routers rather than through the Neutron L3 agent model. Neutron still manages routers and floating IP objects through the API, but the dataplane implementation becomes part of OVN. This means our configuration avoids running neutron-l3-agent for the primary routing path when OVN is in control.

DHCP Agent

The DHCP agent has been a standard component in many Neutron designs, but OVN provides native DHCP for tenant networks. That means we do not rely on neutron-dhcp-agent as a required component for tenant IP assignment in an OVN-first setup. DHCP behavior remains present, but it is delivered by OVN rather than by a separate Neutron DHCP service.

Metadata Agent

Instances still need metadata for SSH keys and user data. OVN provides a dedicated metadata agent integration, so neutron-ovn-metadata-agent becomes the correct choice for metadata delivery. This agent works alongside OVN and Nova metadata settings to keep instance initialization consistent.

LinuxBridge Agent and Open vSwitch Agent

The Linux Bridge and the Open vSwitch agent represent alternative mechanism implementations. Our configuration does not use either of those agent models for dataplane implementation. The Open vSwitch remains present, since OVN uses Open vSwitch for dataplane flows, but we do not run the Neutron Open vSwitch agent as the mechanism driver implementation. This is the key difference that makes the approach OVN-first rather than OVS-agent based.

Configuring Neutron Plugins and Agents

We will configure the ML2 plugin with OVN and we will configure OVN integration so Neutron can create and manage logical networking. To do this, we just make use of the following configuration blocks:

```
[ml2]
type_drivers = flat,vlan,geneve
tenant_network_types = geneve
mechanism_drivers = ovn
extension_drivers = port_security
[ml2_type_vlan]
network_vlan_ranges = physnet1:100:200
[ml2_type_geneve]
vni_ranges = 1000:5000
max_header_size = 38
```

The Bridge mappings move into Open vSwitch configuration, because OVN still uses Open vSwitch bridges to connect provider networks. So here, we need to confirm that the mapping aligns with the physical network and the external bridge:

```
[ovs]
bridge_mappings = physnet1:br-ex
```

We now move on to configuring the OVN connectivity so Neutron can talk to OVN databases. For this, we will edit the **`ovn.ini`** and set the Northbound and Southbound database connections and enable metadata support:

```
[ovn]
ovn_nb_connection = tcp:controller:6641
ovn_sb_connection = tcp:controller:6642
ovn_metadata_enabled = True
```

We will then restart the Neutron server and the OVN metadata agent.

```
sudo systemctl restart neutron-server neutron-ovn-metadata-agent
```

And finally, we will verify the configuration. For this, we will list the network agents and then we create a test network and subnet so Neutron proves it can program OVN logical networking:

```
openstack network agent list
openstack network create test-network
openstack subnet create
  --network test-network
  --subnet-range 10.0.0.0/24 test-subnet
```

With this recipe, we configured Neutron plugins and the OVN components for GitforGits. As a result, we were able to enable network segmentation, routing, and metadata delivery through an OVN-first architecture.This keeps provider networks explicit and tenant networks scalable.

Recipe 3: Deploying OVN and Tenant Networks

In this recipe, we will create a provider network, create a tenant network, connect them through a router, boot two instances, and then verify two traffic patterns that matter in any real cloud setup. Our first traffic pattern is instance to instance communication inside the tenant network, which gives us east west connectivity. Our second traffic pattern is external access to an instance through a floating IP, which gives us north south connectivity.

The key idea is that, when we create a network, subnet, router, or floating IP through the OpenStack CLI, we are defining the intent. The OVN then carries out that intent by building logical switching and routing behavior across Open vSwitch. This distinction matters because it keeps our workflow clean.

Creating Provider Network and External Subnet

In our earlier Neutron setup, we already mapped the provider physical network name to the external bridge, so we will reuse that mapping here.

To start with, we will now create a flat external network called ovn-ext-net, and we attach a subnet that matches the reachable address space in our lab.

```
openstack network create \
  --external \
  --provider-network-type flat \
  --provider-physical-network provider \
  ovn-ext-net
openstack subnet create \
  --network ovn-ext-net \
  --subnet-range 203.0.113.0/24 \
  --allocation-pool start=203.0.113.100,end=203.0.113.200 \
  --dns-nameserver 8.8.8.8 \
  --gateway 203.0.113.1 \
  ovn-ext-subnet
openstack network show ovn-ext-net
openstack subnet show ovn-ext-subnet
```

These commands give us the external side of our topology. The provider network becomes the source for floating IP allocation, and the subnet defines the address pool that Neutron can draw from later.

Creating Tenant Network, Tenant Subnet, and Router

Now, our next step is to create tenant network where our instances will live. This network will use OVN-backed logical switching, and the subnet will provide fixed IP addresses to our workloads.

```
openstack network create ovn-tenant-net
openstack subnet create \
  --network ovn-tenant-net \
  --subnet-range 192.168.10.0/24 \
  --gateway 192.168.10.1 \
```

```
  --dns-nameserver 8.8.8.8 \
  ovn-tenant-subnet
openstack router create ovn-router
openstack router set ovn-router --external-gateway ovn-ext-net
openstack router add subnet ovn-router ovn-tenant-subnet
openstack router show ovn-router
openstack router port list ovn-router
```

At this point, our topology has shape. We have one network that faces outward, one network that hosts workloads, and one router that connects the two.

Booting Two Instances on Tenant Network

We will create two instances named **ovn-vm-1** and **ovn-vm-2** on **ovn-tenant-net**. Since our image and flavor already exist, we will reuse **CirrOS** and **m1.small** in the commands below:

```
openstack server create \
  --flavor m1.small \
  --image CirrOS \
  --network ovn-tenant-net \
  ovn-vm-1
openstack server create \
  --flavor m1.small \
  --image CirrOS \
  --network ovn-tenant-net \
  ovn-vm-2
openstack server list
openstack server show ovn-vm-1 -f value -c addresses
openstack server show ovn-vm-2 -f value -c addresses
```

These two servers gives us the minimum working setup for tenant traffic validation. We have actual ports attached to the tenant network, actual fixed IP addresses assigned through the subnet, and actual compute workloads that must communicate through the OVN-backed dataplane. Once both instances are active and have addresses, we are ready to verify traffic directly.

Validating Instance to Instance Connectivity

We will now prove that our tenant network is working by testing traffic from one instance to the other. So here, we will first make sure ICMP is allowed through the default security group, since a blocked ping can confuse our validation even when the network itself is correct. After that, we will open the console for **ovn-vm-1**, sign in, and ping the fixed IP address of **ovn-vm-2**.

```
openstack security group rule create --protocol icmp --remote-ip 0.0.0.0/0 default
openstack console url show ovn-vm-1
```

Inside the console for **ovn-vm-1**, we then run:

```
ping -c 4 192.168.10.XX
```

If it is a successful ping, it will tell us that the tenant network is alive and that OVN is carrying east west traffic correctly. If ping fails, then we need to inspect the port list and the server address fields, and also to compare the addresses to the expected subnet.

```
openstack port list --network ovn-tenant-net
openstack server show ovn-vm-1 -f value -c status -c addresses
openstack server show ovn-vm-2 -f value -c status -c addresses
```

This validation gives us confidence that the full path is working. Our provider network is supplying floating IP addresses, our router is linking tenant and external segments, and OVN is implementing the logical routing and NAT behavior required to make the instance reachable from outside the tenant network.

Recipe 4: Setting up VLAN and Geneve Overlay

Previously, we explored L2 networking and its various network types supported by Neutron, including VLAN and Geneve. In this recipe, we will create one VLAN network, create one tenant overlay network, attach instances to both, and verify that each network behaves as expected. The OpenStack environment variables, image, flavor, and key pair are already available from the earlier recipes, so herein this recipe, we will limit our focus only on network creation and validation.

Creating VLAN-backed Network

We will start with VLAN-backed network because it is tied directly to the provider network mapping which is already configured in Neutron. This network will use a VLAN segment ID and the physical network name that matches our Open vSwitch bridge mapping. We will create the network, assign a subnet, and launch an instance on it.

Once the instance becomes ACTIVE, it should receive an address from the VLAN subnet and be able to reach the subnet gateway.

Following is the quick network:

```
openstack network create \
  --provider-network-type vlan \
  --provider-physical-network physnet1 \
  --provider-segment 101 \
  --share \
  vlan-network-101
openstack subnet create \
  --network vlan-network-101 \
  --subnet-range 192.168.101.0/24 \
  vlan-subnet-101
openstack server create \
  --flavor m1.small \
  --image CirrOS \
  --network vlan-network-101 \
  --key-name mykey \
  vlan-instance-1
```

After this, we will verify the network objects and the instance address:

```
openstack network show vlan-network-101
openstack subnet show vlan-subnet-101
openstack server show vlan-instance-1 -f value -c addresses
openstack console url show vlan-instance-1
```

Next, inside the guest, we will run the following:

```
ip addr
ping -c 4 192.168.101.1
```

Creating OVN Tenant Overlay Network

Now the second part of this recipe is to create tenant-side L2 network. In this, we will create one overlay network, attach a subnet, and then boot two instances so we can validate instance-to-instance traffic over their fixed IP addresses.

```
openstack network create tenant-overlay-1001
openstack subnet create \
  --network tenant-overlay-1001 \
  --subnet-range 10.0.100.0/24 \
  tenant-overlay-subnet-1001
openstack server create \
  --flavor m1.small \
  --image CirrOS \
  --network tenant-overlay-1001 \
  --key-name mykey \
  overlay-instance-1
openstack server create \
  --flavor m1.small \
  --image CirrOS \
  --network tenant-overlay-1001 \
  --key-name mykey \
  overlay-instance-2
```

Next, we will now inspect the network and instance addresses:

```
openstack network show tenant-overlay-1001
openstack subnet show tenant-overlay-subnet-1001
openstack server show overlay-instance-1 -f value -c addresses
openstack server show overlay-instance-2 -f value -c addresses
openstack console url show overlay-instance-1
```

After this, inside **overlay-instance-1**, we will then ping the fixed IP of **overlay-**

instance-2:

```
ping -c 4 10.0.100.XX
```

At this stage, we have one VLAN-backed network and one OVN-backed tenant overlay network running in the same cloud. The VLAN network gives us a provider-aligned Layer 2 segment, and the overlay network gives us a tenant segment for workload isolation.

Now, the last step is to list the objects we created so we can confirm that Neutron reflects the intended state.

```
openstack network list
openstack subnet list
openstack port list
openstack server list
```

This leaves us with both L2 models ready for the next networking steps.

Recipe 5: Implementing Neutron L3 Routing

In cloud environments, L3 routing is for enabling communication between different networks. The Neutron L3 routing facilitates the routing of traffic between subnets, networks, and external networks, allowing instances on different networks to communicate with each other and with external networks like the internet. This capability connects private networks to external resources, managing floating IPs, and providing internet access to instances.

In this recipe, we will learn to implement Neutron L3 routing. We will configure routers, connect internal networks, set up external networks, and assign floating IPs to instances.

Creating External Network

Now here, before we setup the L3 routing, we need to configure an external network in Neutron. The external network represents the network that provides connectivity to the outside world, such as the internet.

So, to create an external network:

```
openstack network create --external --provider-network-type
flat --provider-physical-network physnet1 external-network
```

Here,

- **--external** marks the network as external.

- **--provider-network-type flat** specifies the network type as flat, which is typical for external networks. And,
- **--provider-physical-network physnet1** maps the network to physical network interface.

Creating Subnet

Next, we then create a subnet for the external network. This subnet should have a range of IP addresses that are routable and accessible from outside the cloud environment.

```
openstack subnet create --network external-network --subnet-
range 203.0.113.0/24 --allocation-pool
start=203.0.113.100,end=203.0.113.200 --gateway 203.0.113.1 --
no-dhcp external-subnet
```

In the above code,

- **--subnet-range 203.0.113.0/24** specifies the IP address range for the external subnet.
- **--allocation-pool** defines the range of IP addresses available for floating IPs.
- **--gateway 203.0.113.1** sets the gateway IP address for the external subnet. And,
- **--no-dhcp** disables DHCP on the external network since external IPs are typically statically assigned.

Configuring Router

Now, the next step is to create a router in Neutron. The router will route traffic between internal networks and the external network. It enables communication between instances on different networks and providing external connectivity.

Following are the steps:

- Create Router

```
openstack router create gitforgits-router
```

It creates a router named **gitforgits-router**.

- Set External Gateway for Router

```
openstack router set gitforgits-router --external-gateway
external-network
```

This then configures the router to use the **external-network** as its gateway.

- Connect Internal Networks to Router

```
openstack router add subnet gitforgits-router vlan-subnet-101

openstack router add subnet gitforgits-router vxlan-subnet-
1001
```

This connects **vlan-subnet-101** and **vxlan-subnet-1001** to **gitforgits-router**.

Assigning Floating IPs to Instances

The floating IPs allow instances on internal networks to be accessible from external networks. This is particularly useful for providing public access to web servers, SSH access to instances, and other use cases where external connectivity is required.

Here is how we do it:

- Allocate Floating IP

```
openstack floating ip create external-network
```

It returns a floating IP address that we can associate with an instance.

- Associate Floating IP with Instance

```
openstack server add floating ip vlan-instance-1 <floating_ip>
```

This thing then makes the **vlan-instance-1** instance accessible from the external network via the floating IP.

- Verify External Connectivity

```
ssh -i mykey.pem ubuntu@<floating_ip>
```

It confirms that the instance is successfully connected to the external network through the router.

Implementing Advanced L3 Features

The Neutron's L3 agent also supports advanced features such as Distributed Virtual Routing (DVR) and High Availability (HA) routers, which can be implemented based on GitforGits' needs.

The implementation is done with following quick steps:

- Enable DVR in ML2 Configuration

```
[ml2]
```

```
mechanism_drivers = openvswitch,l2population
[agent]
enable_distributed_routing = True
l3_ha = True
```

It enables distributed routing and high availability for the L3 agent.

- Enable DVR for Router

```
openstack router create --distributed gitforgits-dvr-router
```

This then creates a router with DVR enabled.

- Configuring HA Routers

```
openstack router create --ha gitforgits-ha-router
```

This command creates a high-availability router.

With this, we can say that, we implemented Neutron L3 routing for communication between internal networks and external networks. All these steps make a seamless and scalable network connectivity for the cloud infrastructure to have secure and efficient communication across all components of the environment.

Recipe 6: Configuring Neutron Security Groups and Firewall Rules

The latest trends in cloud security show that network-based attacks are getting more sophisticated. This includes DDoS attacks, lateral movement within networks, and targeted exploits against cloud instances. You've got to be super careful when setting up security groups and firewall rules. We need to make sure you're limiting the attack surfaces, but still keep things connected. The security best practices now say we should adopt a "**zero trust**" model, where the default posture is to deny all traffic unless it's explicitly permitted. These measures help reduce the chances of unauthorized access and limit the potential damage if there is a breach. Also, more and more cloud environments are using automated tools to manage and enforce security policies across changing and growing infrastructures. This makes sure that security posture stays consistent even as the environment changes.

In this recipe, we're going to take a look at setting up the Neutron security groups and firewall rules. And, we'll put in place the best security practices to keep instances and networks safe from unauthorized access, while making sure that services still work.

Exploring Neutron Security Groups

Generally, the security groups in Neutron are sets of IP filter rules that define the allowed inbound and outbound traffic for instances. And, each instance can be associated with one or more security groups, and the rules within these groups determine what traffic is permitted to and from the instance.

By default, every OpenStack project has a security group named **`default`**. This group allows all outbound traffic but denies all inbound traffic unless explicitly permitted. It is a good practice to modify this group or create custom security groups tailored to specific applications and use cases. It is often useful to create custom security groups that are specific to the roles and functions of different instances. For example, a security group for web servers might allow HTTP and HTTPS traffic, while a security group for database servers might restrict access to only certain IP ranges.

Configuring Neutron Security Groups

Create Custom Security Group

We will first create a custom security group for GitforGits:

```
openstack security group create gitforgits-web-sg --
description "Security group for GitforGits web servers"
```

This creates a security group named **`gitforgits-web-sg`** with a description indicating its purpose.

Add Inbound Rules

Next, we then add rules to allow inbound traffic for HTTP (port 80) and HTTPS (port 443):

```
openstack security group rule create --proto tcp --dst-port 80
--ingress --description "Allow HTTP traffic" gitforgits-web-sg

openstack security group rule create --proto tcp --dst-port
443 --ingress --description "Allow HTTPS traffic" gitforgits-
web-sg
```

This will let pass the inbound HTTP and HTTPS traffic.

Add Outbound Rules

By default, the outbound traffic is usually allowed, but we can explicitly define outbound rules if needed. For example, to restrict outbound traffic to only allow DNS queries:

```
openstack security group rule create --proto udp --dst-port 53
--egress --description "Allow DNS queries" gitforgits-web-sg
```

This rule allows instances in the **gitforgits-web-sg** security group to perform DNS queries.

Associate Security Group with Instance

Finally, we can associate the security group with an instance to apply the rules:

```
openstack server add security group <instance_name>
gitforgits-web-sg
```

This thing then applies the **gitforgits-web-sg** security group to the specified instance.

Configuring Firewall Rules

In addition to security groups, the Neutron can be configured with firewall rules at the network level. And, these rules can be used to control traffic between networks or to implement more granular security policies that complement security groups.

Create Firewall Policy

A firewall policy is a collection of firewall rules that are applied to a network. So here, we will first create a firewall policy:

```
openstack firewall group policy create gitforgits-fw-policy --
description "Firewall policy for GitforGits"
```

This creates a firewall policy named **gitforgits-fw-policy**.

Add Rules to Firewall Policy

The immediate next step is to add rules to the firewall policy to control traffic between networks.

```
openstack firewall rule create --protocol tcp --destination-
port 22 --source-ip-address 192.168.1.0/24 --action allow --
name allow-ssh

openstack firewall group policy insert rule allow-ssh
gitforgits-fw-policy
```

The above script then creates a rule named **allow-ssh** that permits SSH traffic from the **192.168.1.0/24** network and adds it to the **gitforgits-fw-policy**.

Apply Firewall Policy to Network

Finally, we then apply the firewall policy to a network by creating a firewall group and associating it with the policy:

```
openstack firewall group create --ingress-firewall-policy
gitforgits-fw-policy --name gitforgits-fw-group

openstack firewall group set --port <router_port_id>
gitforgits-fw-group
```

This thing will ensure that the traffic passing through the router is filtered according to the firewall policy. To sum up, we learned to configure security groups and firewall rules. And, also to create, manage, and apply these security measures effectively.

Recipe 7: Troubleshooting Neutron Networking Issues

As we've learned through the previous recipes in this chapter, tasks and operations like setting up and configuring Neutron, security groups, and firewall rules, does require careful attention. However, even with the best configurations, issues can arise that disrupt network connectivity or degrade performance.

So, in this recipe, we will explore the common networking issues that might arise while working through all the networking tasks, and will explore the practical, hands-on solutions to prevent and resolve them.

Troubleshooting L2 Networking Issues

VLAN/VXLAN Instances Communication Error

At times, the instances on the same VLAN or VXLAN network are unable to ping each other or access shared services.

And this could be due to:

- Misconfiguration of the VLAN ID or VXLAN Network Identifier (VNI).
- Incorrect physical network mappings or bridge configurations.
- Open vSwitch (OVS) agent not running or misconfigured.

The solution to such issues can be through the following steps:

Verify VLAN/VXLAN Configuration

At first, we need to check that the correct VLAN ID or VNI is configured in Neutron and on the physical switches or routers:

```
openstack network show <network_id>
```

here, we have to verify that the **provider:segmentation_id** matches the expected VLAN ID or VNI.

Check Bridge Mappings

We need to be sure of the OVS bridge mappings are correctly configured on the compute and network nodes:

```
sudo ovs-vsctl show
```

Here, we need to verify that the physical network interfaces are correctly mapped to the OVS bridges (e.g., **br-ex**).

Restart OVS Agent

If the OVS agent is not functioning correctly, we can simply restart it:

```
sudo systemctl restart neutron-openvswitch-agent
```

if not, then we can check **openvswitch-agent.log** for errors.

High Latency/Packet Loss in VXLAN Networks

Sometime, the instances on VXLAN networks experience high latency or intermittent packet loss. And this could be due to:

- CPU overhead due to VXLAN encapsulation.
- Network congestion or insufficient bandwidth.
- Incorrect MTU (Maximum Transmission Unit) settings.

Check MTU Settings

In this case, the VXLAN encapsulation adds overhead to packets, which can cause issues if the MTU is not correctly set. So here, we will verify that the MTU is configured correctly on the VXLAN networks:

```
openstack network show <vxlan_network_id>
```

We need to ascertain that the MTU is set to 1450 or lower to account for the VXLAN overhead.

Troubleshooting L3 Routing Issues

Instances not reaching External Networks

At times, the instances on internal networks are unable to access external networks or the internet, even though a router is configured.

And, this could be due to:

- Misconfiguration of the router's external gateway.
- Incorrect routing tables or missing default route.
- Floating IPs not associated or incorrectly configured.

So here:

Verify Router Configuration

We can check that the router's external gateway is correctly set:

```
openstack router show <router_id>
```

The **`external_gateway_info`** shall point to the correct external network.

Check Routing Tables

On the instance, we may have to check the routing table to ensure that there is a default route pointing to the Neutron router:

```
ip route
```

If the default route is missing, then we need to verify that the DHCP agent is correctly assigning routes.

Test Floating IP Connectivity

If a floating IP is assigned, then we need to check if is correctly associated with the instance:

```
openstack floating ip list
```

The floating IP should be associated with the correct instance and that security groups allow the necessary traffic.

Intermittent Connectivity between Internal Networks

At times, the instances on different internal networks intermittently lose connectivity, or there is a delay in establishing connections. And, this could be due to:

- Issues with the L3 agent or DVR setup.
- Asymmetric routing due to misconfiguration of the external gateway.

- Network congestion or firewall rule conflicts.

So here, the steps could be:

Check L3 Agent Logs

We can review and examine the L3 agent logs for errors or issues related to routing:

```
tail -f /var/log/neutron/l3-agent.log
```

Here, we need to look for any errors related to the router or network interfaces.

Verify DVR Configuration

If using DVR, then we need to check that it is correctly configured on all relevant nodes.

Troubleshooting Security Groups and Firewall Rules

Instances not Accessible

The instances may not be accessible via SSH, HTTP, or other services, even though the security group rules are correctly configured.

And, this may arise due to:

- Misconfigured firewall rules on the host or network nodes.
- Security group rules not applied due to Neutron agent issues.
- Conflicting rules between security groups and firewall policies.

So here, the solution could be:

Verify Security Group Rules

We will double-check the security group rules to ensure they are correctly configured:

```
openstack security group show <security_group_id>
```

And, we will confirm that the necessary inbound and outbound rules are present and correctly specified.

Check Neutron Logs for Errors

We will review the Neutron server and agent logs for any errors related to security group rule application:

```
tail -f /var/log/neutron/neutron-server.log
tail -f /var/log/neutron/iptables-firewall.log
```

And, we will spot any errors that indicate issues with security group rule application.

Blocking Legitimate Traffic

There are also very common issues wherein the legitimate traffic gets blocked by firewall rules. And it thereby prevents the instances from communicating as expected.

And, this could be due to:

- Overly restrictive firewall rules.
- Firewall policy conflicts or misconfigurations.
- Incorrect order of firewall rules leading to unintended blocking.

So here, we can take the following steps:

Review Firewall Policies and Rules

We can check the firewall policies and rules to ensure they are not overly restrictive or conflicting with each other:

```
openstack firewall group policy show <policy_id>
```

Here, we shall review the order of the rules to ensure that allow rules are prioritized correctly.

Temporarily Disable Specific Rules

As a diagnostic step, we can also disable specific firewall rules temporarily to see if the issue resolves. It can help pinpoint which rule is causing the issue:

```
openstack firewall rule delete <rule_id>
```

After identifying the problematic rule, we can adjust it to allow legitimate traffic while maintaining security.

To sum up, in this recipe, we explored solutions for issues around L2 and L3 networking, security groups, and firewall rules. And, all these troubleshooting skills are must for quickly resolving any issues that may arise.

Recipe 8: OVN Operations with Neutron and OVN CLI Tools

While the Neutron handles networking side of things, the OVN does all the switching and routing. Hence, when it comes to keeping an eye on things, we need to check OVN northbound and southbound databases, logical switches and logical routers, and also we need to confirm that the local Open vSwitch dataplane is attached to the expected bridges.

So, in this recipe, we'll be working directly with OVN CLI tools to see how Neutron objects appear inside OVN. We'll check the logical switches and routers, make sure the chassis registration is correct, and then set up a test network and subnet.

Preparing OVN Operational View

What we need now is a structured way to inspect the running state of OVN. The three most useful starting points are:

- the OVN Northbound database,
- the OVN Southbound database, and
- the local Open vSwitch configuration.

The Northbound database shows the logical intent such as switches, routers, ports, and NAT rules. The Southbound database shows how that intent is distributed to chassis. And, the Open vSwitch shows the local bridge and port state on the node.

So here, we will now run the following commands to give us a baseline view of OVN before we create or inspect any new networking objects.

```
ovn-nbctl show
ovn-sbctl show
ovs-vsctl show
```

These three commands should already return meaningful output if OVN is active. The **ovn-nbctl** show should list logical switches and routers, **ovn-sbctl** show should list chassis and datapath details, and **ovs-vsctl** show should display bridges such as **br-int** and any provider-facing bridge already mapped in our environment.

Inspecting Logical Networks and Routers

Next, we are looking for the expected switch names, router names, connected ports, and any NAT information that supports floating IP traffic. To do this, run the following command and review the output:

```
ovn-nbctl ls-list
ovn-nbctl lr-list
ovn-nbctl lsp-list ovn-tenant-net
ovn-nbctl lr-nat-list ovn-router
```

If the exact switch or router name differs in your environment, then we need to substitute the correct object name from **ovn-nbctl** show.

Creating Test Network and Verifying OVN Programming

We will now create a small Neutron network and subnet so we can observe how a new object appears in OVN immediately after creation. It will keep our workflow hands-on and helps us connect Neutron commands to OVN backend state.

```
openstack network create ovn-ops-net

openstack subnet create --network ovn-ops-net --subnet-range 10.20.30.0/24 ovn-ops-subnet

openstack network show ovn-ops-net

ovn-nbctl ls-list

ovn-nbctl lsp-list ovn-ops-net
```

After this, the Neutron network should now exist in both views. The OpenStack command confirms the API object, and the OVN commands confirm the backend logical switch. If the Neutron object exists but the OVN object does not, the issue is likely between Neutron and OVN rather than inside the dataplane.

Checking Chassis and Dataplane Health

Our final step is to confirm that OVN chassis registration and local dataplane health are in a usable state. The chassis entries, in general, shows us which nodes are participating in OVN, and the Open vSwitch bridges show whether the integration bridge and external bridge are present. This is often the first place to check when ports bind but traffic does not flow.

So for this, we will run the following commands and review the chassis names, encapsulation details, and bridge list.

```
ovn-sbctl chassis-list

ovn-sbctl show

ovs-vsctl show

openstack network list

openstack subnet list
```

With these steps, we can say that we have a working operational workflow for OVN-backed Neutron networking.

Summary

In this chapter, we learned Neutron networking in an OVN-first OpenStack environment. We began learning the main OpenStack network types and understanding where provider networks and tenant networks fit into GitforGits environment. We then configured ML2 plugin and OVN components with OVN as the backend for switching, routing, metadata handling, and tenant isolation.

Next, we then moved into actual network deployment and operations. We created provider networks and tenant networks, connected them through routing, and validated both instance-to-instance traffic and north-south connectivity with floating IPs. We also worked through Layer 2 networking with VLAN-backed segments and Geneve-based overlay networks to understand the physical mapping and logical tenant isolation in single cloud. Finally, we learned to work with OVN operationally by using OVN CLI tools to inspect logical switches, logical routers, ports, chassis state, and backend programming. By the end, we got into real working cloud connectivity and gained operational view of Neutron and OVN functioning together in daily OpenStack administration.

Chapter 5: Resource Computing with Nova

Introduction

In this chapter, we will look at core of OpenStack compute resources by exploring the capabilities of Nova. The goal of this chapter is to learn the tools we need to manage and scale instances in the OpenStack environment, as well as deploy them.

Every OpenStack administrator is expected to know to use Nova for launching the virtual machine instances, and that's where we will start this chapter. Next, we then manage instance placement and affinity rules so that we can optimize the resource usage. We will then go over deploying instances with SSH key injection for securing access to the virtual machines. The next section covers Nova hypervisors and to use different hypervisors, such as KVM and QEMU, to control the execution and management of instances. And lastly, we will learn to set up Nova for resource quotas and limits, ensuring that the cloud environment remains efficient and within operational parameters.

Recipe 1: Launching Virtual Machine Instances with Nova

Nova is the core compute service, and it is responsible for managing the lifecycle of virtual machine (VM) instances. It acts as the primary interface between the cloud's compute resources and the users who need to deploy and manage these VMs. For GitforGits, the Nova offers on-demand provisioning of instances, automated resource scheduling, and seamless integration with Neutron for networking and Cinder for storage.

Hence, in this recipe, we will focus on launching virtual machine instances using Nova. We'll go through the practical steps required to deploy a VM instance, including selecting an appropriate flavor, configuring network connectivity, and ensuring secure access via SSH. These tasks are very much fundamental for managing compute resources and thereby it forms the foundation for advanced operations with Nova.

We will now proceed to the following steps:

Selecting Flavor

A flavor in OpenStack defines the compute, memory, and storage capacity of a virtual machine instance. The selection of the right flavor matches the resource needs of different workloads.

List Flavors

To see the flavors available in the OpenStack environment:

```
openstack flavor list
```

In it, we review the output to select a flavor that meets the needs of the workload. For example, **m1.small** might be a suitable flavor for a development server with minimal resource requirements.

Create Custom Flavor

If none of the existing flavors meet the requirements, we can create a custom flavor:

```
openstack flavor create --ram 4096 --vcpus 2 --disk 20 custom-flavor
```

It creates a flavor with 4 GB of RAM, 2 VCPUs, and 20 GB of disk space.

Launching VM Instance

With the flavor selected, we can then launch a VM instance using Nova.

Launch Instance

Now, to create a new VM instance:

```
openstack server create --flavor m1.small --image <image_id> --network <network_id> --key-name mykey --security-group <security_group_name> gitforgits-instance1
```

This instructs Nova to create a new virtual machine instance using the specified flavor, image, and network.

Monitor Instance Launch

After issuing the command, we will monitor the status of the instance to ensure it launches successfully:

```
openstack server list
```

The status should change from **BUILD** to **ACTIVE**, indicating that the instance has been successfully launched.

Accessing Instance

Once the instance is active, we can access it via SSH using the key pair specified during the instance creation.

Retrieve Instance's IP Address

Here, we will use the **openstack server list** command to retrieve the IP address assigned to the instance:

```
openstack server list
```

In this, we must note the IP address associated with the instance under **Networks** column.

SSH into Instance

We will now access the instance using SSH:

```
ssh -i mykey.pem ubuntu@<instance_ip>
```

If the image uses a different default user (e.g., **centos** for CentOS images), then we will adjust the SSH command accordingly.

Checking Instance Functionality

Once we are logged in, we can verify if the instance has been allocated the correct resources (CPU, RAM, disk) based on the selected flavor:

```
free -m
df -h
lscpu
```

This will provide details about the memory, disk space, and CPU configuration of the instance.

With these steps, we can say that we have successfully deployed a virtual machine instance, and we can proceed to more advanced Nova functionalities.

Recipe 2: Managing Instance Placement and Affinity Rules

Now that we have successfully launched a VM instance, we can proceed to explore controlling the placement of these instances on the available compute nodes. And thereby, topics like instance placement strategies and affinity rules we will be exploring to.

Affinity and Anti-Affinity Rules

The affinity and anti-affinity rules are policies that guide how instances are placed on physical hosts within the OpenStack environment. These rules are quite essential for optimizing resource utilization, improving performance, and ensuring fault tolerance.

- The affinity rules ensure that certain instances are placed on the same host. This is useful in scenarios where instances need to be close to each other to reduce latency, share resources, or communicate more efficiently.
- Whereas, the anti-affinity rules, on the other hand, ensure that certain instances are placed on different hosts. This is necessary for high availability and fault tolerance, as it prevents a single point of failure. For example, if two instances are critical to an application, placing them on different hosts ensures that if one host fails, the other instance remains unaffected.

Both these rules can allow us to manage its infrastructure more effectively, whether it's by ensuring that critical services are distributed across multiple hosts or by placing related services together to minimize network latency.

Instance Placement Strategies

Before diving into the practical implementation, we will also get used to the instance placement strategies. Now, these placement strategies are dictated by scheduler hints, which are key-value pairs that influence where an instance will be placed. And, these hints can be used to enforce both affinity and anti-affinity rules.

- Scheduler hints are additional metadata that can be passed during the instance creation process. These hints inform the Nova scheduler about specific placement preferences.
- The placement decisions can also be influenced by setting metadata on host aggregates (groups of compute nodes) to ensure that instances are placed on nodes that meet certain criteria, such as having specific hardware characteristics or being in a particular data center.

Implementing Affinity Rules

So, we will begin place the set of instances working closely together on the same compute node to reduce latency.

Creating Affinity Group

The Nova supports the concept of server groups to apply affinity or anti-affinity policies. For this, we will now create an affinity group:

```
openstack server group create --policy affinity gitforgits-
affinity-group
```

It creates a server group named **gitforgits-affinity-group** with an affinity policy, meaning that all instances added to this group will be placed on the same compute node.

Launching Instances with Affinity

While launching the instances that should adhere to this affinity policy, we need to specify the server group too, using the **--hint** option:

```
openstack server create --flavor m1.small --image <image_id> --network <network_id> --key-name mykey --security-group <security_group_name> --hint group=<server_group_id> gitforgits-web-instance1
```

After this, we then launch another instance in the same group to see them placed on the same host:

```
openstack server create --flavor m1.small --image <image_id> --network <network_id> --key-name mykey --security-group <security_group_name> --hint group=<server_group_id> gitforgits-app-instance1
```

Now, both instances will be scheduled to the same host, adhering to the affinity policy.

Verifying Affinity Placement

To verify that the instances have been placed on the same compute node, we can use the **openstack server show** command to check the **OS-EXT-SRV-ATTR:host** attribute for both instances:

```
openstack server show gitforgits-web-instance1

openstack server show gitforgits-app-instance1
```

After this, both the instances show same host under the **OS-EXT-SRV-ATTR:host** attribute, which confirms us that they were placed together.

Implementing Anti-Affinity Rules

Now, we will assume that we need to deploy instances that provide redundancy for critical services, such as two database instances. This means we want to have high availability, so for this, these instances should be placed on different compute nodes.

Creating Anti-Affinity Group

Like affinity, we will create a server group with an anti-affinity policy:

```
openstack server group create --policy anti-affinity gitforgits-anti-affinity-group
```

This creates a server group named **gitforgits-anti-affinity-group** with an anti-affinity policy.

Launching Instances with Anti-Affinity

When launching instances that should adhere to this anti-affinity policy, we will specify the server group in the **--hint** option:

```
openstack server create --flavor m1.small --image <image_id> -
-network <network_id> --key-name mykey --security-group
<security_group_name> --hint group=<server_group_id>
gitforgits-db-instance1
```

Next, we then launch another instance in the same group, just to ensure that they are placed on different hosts:

```
openstack server create --flavor m1.small --image <image_id> -
-network <network_id> --key-name mykey --security-group
<security_group_name> --hint group=<server_group_id>
gitforgits-db-instance2
```

After this, these instances will be placed on different hosts, subject to the anti-affinity policy.

Verifying Anti-Affinity Placement

Similar to the affinity policy, we can also verify that the instances are placed on different hosts by checking the **OS-EXT-SRV-ATTR:host** attribute:

```
openstack server show gitforgits-db-instance1

openstack server show gitforgits-db-instance2
```

The **OS-EXT-SRV-ATTR:host** attribute should show different hosts for each instance, confirming that the anti-affinity policy is in effect.

Managing Affinity Rules

Once affinity or anti-affinity rules are set, there might be a need to modify or delete these rules as the infrastructure evolves.

Revising Server Group Policies

If we need to change the policy of an existing server group (e.g., from affinity to anti-affinity), then we will create a new server group with the desired policy, as policies cannot be changed once set.

```
openstack server group create --policy anti-affinity
gitforgits-revised-group
```

Then, migrate the instances from the old group to the new group by re-launching them under the new group.

If we need to add or remove instances from a server group, this can be done by launching new instances with the desired group or deleting instances that should no longer adhere to the group's policy.

Adding Instance

Here, we will launch a new instance with the desired server group:

```
openstack server create --flavor m1.small --image <image_id> --network <network_id> --key-name mykey --security-group <security_group_name> --hint group=<server_group_id> gitforgits-new-instance
```

Removing Instance

Now, to remove an instance from a server group, we will need to delete it and re-launch it without the **`--hint`** option or with a different group.

If a server group is no longer needed, we can delete it:

```
openstack server group delete <server_group_id>
```

But, note that it does not automatically affect the placement of instances that were created under this group.

Advanced Placement Strategies

In addition to affinity and anti-affinity rules, the Nova do allow for more granular control over instance placement using host aggregates and availability zones.

- Host aggregates allow us to group compute nodes with similar characteristics (e.g., SSD storage, high memory) and apply metadata to these groups. You can then use this metadata to influence where instances are placed based on their resource needs. And,
- Availability zones are logical groupings of hosts that provide an additional layer of fault tolerance. Instances can be placed in different availability zones to ensure they are isolated from failures in other zones.

Creating Host Aggregate

We can create a host aggregate and assign metadata to it:

```
openstack aggregate create gitforgits-ssd-aggregate
```

```
openstack aggregate set --property ssd=true gitforgits-ssd-aggregate
```

After this, we then add hosts to this aggregate:

```
openstack aggregate add host gitforgits-ssd-aggregate <host_name>
```

The instances with specific requirements can now be scheduled to this aggregate by specifying the appropriate metadata in the scheduler hints.

Using Availability Zones

Here, we will create an availability zone and place instances accordingly:

```
openstack availability zone list
```

We then launch instances in a specific availability zone by specifying the zone:

```
openstack server create --flavor m1.small --image <image_id> --availability-zone <zone_name> --network <network_id> --key-name mykey --security-group <security_group_name> gitforgits-zone-instance
```

After this, the instance gets placed within the desired availability zone.

To sum up, we launched VM instances, introduced server groups, implemented rules to optimize performance and high availability, and learned to modify and delete the rules.

Recipe 3: Using Placement API for Scheduling Visibility

The Placement API gives us a direct way to understand how Nova views available capacity before an instance is scheduled. When we create a server, the Nova scheduler does not choose a host blindly. It queries Placement for allocation candidates, checks inventories such as **`VCPU`**, **`MEMORY_MB`**, and **`DISK_GB`**, considers host traits, and then records allocations for the selected destination. Instead of guessing why a workload did or did not land on a host, it queries the Placement and observe what Nova saw at scheduling time. And, this makes the Placement very useful for real operational troubleshooting when builds fail, when capacity appears exhausted, or when a host that looks healthy from the outside is silently filtered out by the scheduler.

In this recipe, we will begin collecting the two values we need for direct Placement API work as follows:

Preparing Token and Placement Endpoint

To begin with, we need a valid Keystone token, and Placement endpoint URL from service catalog. Now, we can obtain both of them using OpenStack CLI. Once we have those values, we can query Placement with curl and format the output through Python.

```
TOKEN=$(openstack token issue -f value -c id)

PLACEMENT=$(openstack endpoint list --service placement --
interface public -f value -c URL)
```

Listing Resource Providers

Our first Placement query will list resource providers, and these providers typically represent compute nodes, and they form the scheduling targets that Nova can place workloads on. The returned data includes names and UUIDs, and we will reuse one UUID in later calls. The point of this step is not only to get an identifier. So here, the point is to confirm that Placement knows about our compute resources and that the scheduling landscape is visible from the API side.

```
curl -s -H "X-Auth-Token: $TOKEN" \

  -H "OpenStack-API-Version: placement 1.39" \

  "$PLACEMENT/resource_providers" | python3 -m json.tool
```

After this, we will choose one provider UUID from the output and keep it in a shell variable:

```
RP_UUID=<resource_provider_uuid>
```

Inspecting Inventories

The inventories tell us what raw capacity a resource provider is advertising. It usually includes virtual CPUs, memory in megabytes, and disk capacity. And, these values are what Nova scheduler evaluates when deciding whether a host can satisfy a flavor request.

```
curl -s -H "X-Auth-Token: $TOKEN" \

  -H "OpenStack-API-Version: placement 1.39" \

  "$PLACEMENT/resource_providers/$RP_UUID/inventories" |
python3 -m json.tool
```

Inspecting Traits and Allocations

Traits describe host capabilities. A host may advertise standard traits or custom traits depending on its hardware and configuration. These traits become especially useful when we want workloads to land only on hosts with certain characteristics. Even if we are not yet using custom traits heavily, seeing them at the Placement level helps us understand how host specialization becomes visible to the scheduler.

```
curl -s -H "X-Auth-Token: $TOKEN" \
  -H "OpenStack-API-Version: placement 1.39" \
  "$PLACEMENT/resource_providers/$RP_UUID/traits" | python3 -m
json.tool
```

Now the allocations show us what portion of a provider's advertised resources is already consumed by running workloads. This is the real link between capacity and actual scheduling activity. A host may advertise inventory, but allocations tell us how much of that inventory is already spoken for.

```
curl -s -H "X-Auth-Token: $TOKEN" \
  -H "OpenStack-API-Version: placement 1.39" \
  "$PLACEMENT/resource_providers/$RP_UUID/allocations" |
python3 -m json.tool
```

Launching Test Instance

After this, we will connect Placement visibility to a real Nova event. Here, we will launch a small test instance and then query allocations again. It will give us a before-and-after view that ties Nova scheduling directly to Placement state.

```
openstack server create \
  --flavor m1.small \
  --image CirrOS \
  --network ovn-tenant-net \
  placement-test-vm


openstack server list
openstack server show placement-test-vm -f value -c status -c
OS-EXT-SRV-ATTR:host
```

Rechecking Allocations after Scheduling

Now that the instance is active, we query allocations again and compare the result with the earlier output. This is the most useful part of the recipe because it shows us how Placement changes in response to actual workload placement. We are no longer only reading static host data. We are here watching how the scheduling becomes visible through the API.

```
curl -s -H "X-Auth-Token: $TOKEN" \
  -H "OpenStack-API-Version: placement 1.39" \
  "$PLACEMENT/resource_providers/$RP_UUID/allocations" |
python3 -m json.tool
```

With this, we have a repeatable method for making Nova scheduling visible. We can list resource providers, inspect inventories, inspect traits, and observe allocations before and after a server build. That gives us a practical operational lens into compute placement. From this point onward, when a workload lands on an unexpected host or fails to schedule, we do not need to guess. We can move directly into Placement and verify what capacity, traits, and allocation state existed at the moment of scheduling.

Recipe 4: Managing GPU Workloads

Not every computer can handle GPU workloads, so they need special scheduling. A normal flavor that only needs CPU, memory, and disk can be placed on many hosts, but a GPU-enabled workload needs to land on a host that actually has the required device capability. Nova handles this by combining host-side PCI or vGPU preparation with placement-aware scheduling. All we have to do is make the GPU visible to Nova, define a reusable alias for it, and then request that alias through a flavor. Once that's set up, we can ask Placement for a host that meets the request instead of treating the GPU requirement as an afterthought.

Preparing Compute Host

So here, we begin on the compute node because that is where the physical device exists. The operating system and hypervisor are assumed to be ready for passthrough or vGPU use already. Our focus here is Nova configuration. In **/etc/nova/nova.conf**, we will define the device specification, define an alias, and enable reporting into Placement.

```
# Compute node: /etc/nova/nova.conf
[pci]
device_spec = { "vendor_id":"10de", "product_id":"25b6",
"address":"0000:25:00.4" }
alias = { "vendor_id":"10de", "product_id":"25b6",
"device_type":"type-PF", "name":"gpu1" }
```

```
report_in_placement = true
```

Preparing Controller

The controller services also need to understand the alias so that flavor requests are interpreted correctly. So here, we will enable PCI-aware placement scheduling on the controller side.

```
# Controller services: /etc/nova/nova.conf
[pci]
alias = { "vendor_id":"10de", "product_id":"25b6",
"device_type":"type-PF", "name":"gpu1" }

[filter_scheduler]
pci_in_placement = true
```

After saving the configuration, we will then restart the affected Nova services so the new alias and reporting behavior become active.

```
sudo systemctl restart nova-compute
sudo systemctl restart nova-api nova-scheduler nova-conductor
```

Creating GPU Flavor

Before we request a GPU workload, we will verify that Nova services still report healthy status. It gives us a clean checkpoint before we move into flavor-based scheduling.

```
openstack compute service list
openstack hypervisor list
```

After this, we will create a new flavor and attach the GPU alias through the **pci_passthrough:alias** property. It makes the flavor GPU-aware and gives Nova scheduler a clear requirement to satisfy when placing the server.

```
openstack flavor create gpu.small --ram 4096 --disk 20 --vcpus
4
openstack flavor set gpu.small --property
"pci_passthrough:alias"="gpu1:1"
```

Launching GPU Workload

We will now boot a server with the GPU-enabled flavor. This is where all the earlier preparation comes together. The scheduler must find a host that advertises the required GPU capability, and the resulting workload should land only on a node that can satisfy that request.

```
openstack server create \
  --flavor gpu.small \
  --image CirrOS \
  --network ovn-tenant-net \
  gpu-test-vm
```

Verifying Host

Once the server becomes ACTIVE, we inspect the host where it landed. It confirms that Nova did not simply place it on any compute node. It placed it on a host capable of satisfying the GPU request. We also list hypervisors so we can compare the selected host against the available compute inventory.

```
openstack server show gpu-test-vm -f value -c status -c OS-
EXT-SRV-ATTR:host
openstack hypervisor list
```

With all the above steps, we have a complete GPU workload path in Nova. This recipe gives us a clean method for accelerator-aware scheduling and prepares our compute layer for specialized workloads that go beyond standard virtual machine placement.

Recipe 5: Deploying Instances with SSH Key Injection

SSH Keys Overview

The SSH (Secure Shell) key injection is a fundamental security practice when deploying VM instances in cloud environments. The use of SSH keys rather than passwords for instance access is highly recommended due to the enhanced security and convenience it offers.

In general, an SSH key pair consists of a public key and a private key. The public key is injected into the instance at the time of creation, while the private key remains with the user. This setup eliminates the need for password authentication, making it much harder for attackers to gain unauthorized access.

The main advantages of using SSH keys are:

- Unlike passwords, which can be guessed or brute-forced, SSH keys provide a much stronger form of authentication. The private key is never exposed to the network, and since it is typically stored securely on the user's machine, the risk of compromise is significantly reduced.
- Once SSH key pairs are set up, users can access their instances without needing to enter a password. This is particularly useful in environments where multiple instances need to be accessed or managed frequently. Additionally, the SSH keys facilitate automation, allowing scripts and tools to interact with instances securely and without manual intervention.
- In cloud environments, managing SSH keys centrally through services like OpenStack makes it easier to enforce security policies and manage access control. The administrators can quickly revoke or update keys across multiple instances, reducing the risk of unauthorized access.

Given these benefits, the SSH key injection is vital for deploying instances securely in GitforGits. Hence, in this recipe, we will learn to deploy instances with SSH key injection using Nova, so that all the instances are accessible securely and efficiently.

Creating SSH Key Pair

Before deploying an instance with SSH key injection, we need to generate an SSH key pair. If we already have an SSH key pair, we can skip this step.

Generate SSH Key Pair

On the local machine, we can generate a new SSH key pair using:

```
ssh-keygen -t rsa -b 4096 -C "gitforgits-key"
```

It generates a 4096-bit RSA key pair. During the process, we will be prompted to specify a file name and location to save the key. The default location is **~/.ssh/id_rsa**. We can name the key **gitforgits-key** or any other name we prefer.

After the key pair is generated, we will have two files:

- **~/.ssh/gitforgits-key** is the private key, which should be kept secure and never shared. And,
- **~/.ssh/gitforgits-key.pub** is the public key, which can be distributed and injected into instances.

Upload Public Key

The next step is to upload the public key to OpenStack, so it can be used during instance deployment:

```
openstack keypair create --public-key ~/.ssh/gitforgits-
key.pub gitforgits-key
```

This then uploads the public key to OpenStack under the name **`gitforgits-key`**. It will now be available for use when launching instances.

Launching Instance with SSH Key Injection

With the SSH key pair ready and uploaded to OpenStack, we can now launch an instance with SSH key injection.

Launch Instance

We then run the following to create a new VM instance with the SSH key injected:

```
openstack server create --flavor m1.small --image <image_id> -
-network <network_id> --key-name gitforgits-key --security-
group <security_group_name> gitforgits-ssh-instance
```

It tells Nova to launch the instance with the **`gitforgits-key`** injected, allowing us to access the instance securely via SSH.

Monitor Instance Launch

After issuing the command, monitor the status of the instance to ensure it launches successfully:

```
openstack server list
```

The status should change from **`BUILD`** to **`ACTIVE`**, indicating that the instance has been successfully launched.

Accessing Instance via SSH

Once the instance is active, we can access it using the SSH key pair we configured.

Retrieve Instance's IP Address

We can use **`openstack server list`** to retrieve the IP address assigned to the instance:

```
openstack server list
```

Here, the IP address is associated with the instance under the **`Networks`** column.

SSH Instance

We can access the instance through the following:

```
ssh -i ~/.ssh/gitforgits-key ubuntu@<instance_ip>
```

If the connection is successful, we will have secure shell access to the instance, ready for further configuration and management.

Managing SSH Keys

At a later period, we may need to manage multiple SSH keys, update keys, or revoke access for certain users. So here, the OpenStack provides quite straightforward commands for it.

Listing SSH Keys

To list all SSH keys associated with the OpenStack account, we can run the following:

```
openstack keypair list
```

It displays all the key pairs we have uploaded to OpenStack, along with their names and associated fingerprints.

Deleting SSH Key

If an SSH key is no longer needed or if we want to revoke access, we can delete it using:

```
openstack keypair delete gitforgits-key
```

It removes the **`gitforgits-key`** from OpenStack. And, any instances that were launched with this key will no longer have access via SSH unless another key is added or the instance is recreated.

With these quick learnings, we explored to generate an SSH key pair, then uploading it to OpenStack, and later to launch instance the SSH key injected. It also covered to access instance securely via SSH and manage SSH keys within OpenStack.

Recipe 6: Using Nova Hypervisors (KVM, QEMU)

KVM and QEMU Overview

The hypervisor is the core component that allows the creation and management of virtual machines (VMs). Nova interfaces with various hypervisors to deploy and manage these VMs. Two of the most widely used hypervisors in OpenStack environments are KVM (Kernel-based Virtual Machine) and QEMU (Quick Emulator).

- KVM is a full virtualization solution for Linux on x86 hardware containing virtualization extensions (Intel VT or AMD-V). It converts Linux kernel into a hypervisor, allowing it to run multiple isolated virtual environments called guests or VMs. It is integrated directly into the Linux kernel, and hence it a popular choice for OpenStack deployments due to its performance, stability, and strong security features. It requires hardware support for virtualization, which is available in most modern CPUs.
- QEMU is a generic and open-source machine emulator and virtualizer. When used in conjunction with KVM, QEMU provides the emulation of hardware devices and enables the execution of guest code at near-native speed. It can operate in two modes: as a full emulator (where it simulates a full system) or as a hypervisor (when paired with KVM). Its versatility makes it a valuable tool in scenarios where full hardware emulation is necessary, although it is typically slower when running in pure emulation mode compared to KVM.

So here, in this recipe, we will learn to utilize KVM and QEMU within GitforGits OpenStack environment so that we can have the infrastructure optimized for performance, scalability, and flexibility.

Verifying Hypervisor Support

Before using KVM or QEMU, it's important to verify that the environment supports these hypervisors and that the necessary components are installed.

So, to check if the system supports hardware virtualization, we run the following:

```
egrep -c '(vmx|svm)' /proc/cpuinfo
```

If the output is greater than 0, the CPU supports hardware virtualization, which is required for KVM.

After this, we then check if the KVM modules are loaded in the kernel:

```
lsmod | grep kvm
```

Here, we should see **kvm** and **kvm_intel** (or **kvm_amd** for AMD processors) listed. If not, we may need to load the modules manually:

```
sudo modprobe kvm
sudo modprobe kvm_intel  # or kvm_amd for AMD processors
```

And then, we will verify that QEMU is installed on the compute nodes:

```
qemu-system-x86_64 --version
```

If QEMU is not installed, we can install it using the package manager:

```
sudo apt-get install qemu-kvm libvirt-bin bridge-utils virt-
manager
```

This installs QEMU along with KVM and other necessary tools.

Configuring Nova for KVM and QEMU

The Nova needs to be configured to use KVM or QEMU as the hypervisor for launching instances. So, we will open the **nova.conf** on the compute node and will apply the following settings:

```
sudo nano /etc/nova/nova.conf
```

In the **[libvirt]** section, we will configure the hypervisor type:

```
[libvirt]
virt_type = kvm  # Use 'qemu' if KVM is not supported or
required
cpu_mode = host-passthrough
```

Here, within **virt_type**, we will set it to **kvm** to use KVM. If the hardware does not support KVM, we can set this to **qemu** for full emulation.

After this, we will then restart the Nova compute service to apply the changes:

```
sudo systemctl restart nova-compute
```

This will confirm that the changes take effect and Nova is now using the configured hypervisor.

Launching Instances with KVM and QEMU

With the hypervisor configured, we can now launch instances using Nova. By default, the Nova will use the hypervisor configured on the compute node.

Launch Instance

We will first launch a new instance:

```
openstack server create --flavor m1.small --image <image_id> --network <network_id> --key-name gitforgits-key --security-group <security_group_name> gitforgits-kvm-instance
```

Verify Hypervisor

After the instance is launched, we then verify that it is running on the correct hypervisor by checking the instance's details:

```
openstack server show gitforgits-kvm-instance
```

Here, we will look for the **OS-EXT-SRV-ATTR:hypervisor_hostname** attribute, which should match the name of the compute node using the configured hypervisor.

Access Instance

Once the instance is active, we then access it via SSH to ensure that it is functioning correctly:

```
ssh -i ~/.ssh/gitforgits-key ubuntu@<instance_ip>
```

With this, we explored the roles of KVM and QEMU as hypervisors, learned the process of verifying hypervisor support, configuring Nova to use KVM or QEMU, and launching instances with these hypervisors.

Recipe 7: Configuring Nova for Resource Quotas and Limits

Resource quotas and limits are required for managing and controlling the allocation of compute resources across different projects. The quotas ensure that no single project or user can consume all available resources, thereby maintaining a balanced and fair usage of the cloud infrastructure.

In this recipe, we will learn to configure and manage resource quotas and limits. We will also learn to allocate these resources project-wise, such that each project within GitforGits has access to the necessary resources without exceeding the overall capacity of the cloud.

Default Quotas

The OpenStack comes with a set of default quotas that apply to all projects unless overridden. These quotas include limits on the number of instances, vCPUs, RAM, floating IPs, and other resources.

To view the default quotas in Nova:

```
openstack quota show --default
```

It will display the default quotas for various resources such as instances, cores (vCPUs), RAM, and more as shown below:

Field	Value
cores	20
instances	10
ram	51200
floating_ips	10
security_groups	10
security_group_rules	100

These values represent the maximum resources that any single project can consume by default.

Configuring Custom Quotas

Now, to tailor resource allocation, we can modify the default quotas on a per-project basis.

For this, we will need to identify the project for which we want to set custom quotas:

```
openstack project list
```

It will display a list of projects along with their IDs, which we will need for the next steps.

Now, to set custom quotas for a specific project, we will run:

```
openstack quota set --cores 50 --instances 25 --ram 102400 --
floating-ips 20 --security-groups 20 <project_id>
```

This above command sets custom quotas for the specified project. These quotas override the default values for this project.

After setting the custom quotas, we verify them using:

```
openstack quota show <project_id>
```

It displays the current quotas for the specified project, confirming that the custom quotas have been applied.

Managing Quota Allocations across Multiple Projects

In a multi-tenant environment, it's demanding to manage quota allocations across multiple projects to ensure fair resource distribution and avoid overallocation.

List Quotas for All Projects

To get an overview of quota allocations across all projects, we can use the following script or loop in the OpenStack environment:

```
for project in $(openstack project list -f value -c ID); do
    echo "Quotas for project $project:"
    openstack quota show $project
    echo "-----------------------------"
done
```

This loop iterates through all projects and displays their quotas, helping us assess the resource distribution.

Adjust Quotas Based on Usage

If certain projects are consistently underutilizing or overutilizing their quotas, we may need to adjust their allocations. You can use the **`openstack quota set`** command to increase or decrease quotas based on actual usage patterns.

For example, to reduce the RAM quota for a project that is underutilizing its allocated memory:

```
openstack quota set --ram 51200 <project_id>
```

It reduces the RAM quota to 50 GB for the specified project.

In some cases, we may want to enforce hard limits on resource usage to prevent projects from requesting additional resources. OpenStack does this automatically based on the quotas we set. If a project tries to exceed its allocated resources, Nova will deny the request, ensuring that no project can consume more than its fair share of resources.

Monitoring Quota Usage

To effectively manage resources, it's important to monitor quota usage regularly. This allows us to anticipate when a project might need additional resources or when limits should be tightened.

The following monitors the quota usage for a specific project:

```
openstack usage show <project_id>
```

It provides detailed information about the project's resource usage, including the number of instances, vCPUs, RAM, and more.

For a more detailed view over a specific time, we can use:

```
openstack usage list --project <project_id> --start
<start_date> --end <end_date>
```

In the above, we need to replace **<start_date>** and **<end_date>** with the desired time range in **YYYY-MM-DD** format to get help in tracking resource consumption trends over time.

Setting Global Quotas

In some cases, we may want to set or adjust global quotas that apply to all projects unless overridden. We can use the following to set global quotas:

```
openstack quota set --cores 1000 --instances 500 --ram 204800
--floating-ips 50 --security-groups 50 --default
```

This then sets new global default quotas for all projects:

- **--cores 1000** limits total vCPUs across all projects.
- **--instances 500** limits the total number of instances across all projects.
- **--ram 204800** limits total RAM across all projects to 200 GB. And,
- **--floating-ips 50** limits the number of floating IPs across all projects.

Recipe 8: Automating Instance Deployments

Manually deploying instances, as we've done in previous recipes, provides a deep understanding of the process and control over individual configurations. However, in a production environment where scalability and efficiency are key, automation becomes a need.

The Nova CLI offers powerful tools for automating these deployments and with the help of scripting commands and using Nova's batch capabilities, we can streamline the process of launching instances, managing configurations, and scaling resources. So here, in this recipe, we'll learn to automate the deployment of instances that were previously deployed manually. We'll also learn to automate the deployment of multiple instances simultaneously for environments requiring quick scaling or load balancing.

Scripting Single Instance Deployment

To begin with, we'll automate the deployment of a single instance using the Nova CLI. This script **deploy_instance.sh** will replicate the manual steps we performed earlier, but in an automated and repeatable manner.

```
nano deploy_instance.sh
```

```
#!/bin/bash

# Variables
IMAGE_ID="<image_id>"
FLAVOR="m1.small"
NETWORK_ID="<network_id>"
KEY_NAME="gitforgits-key"
SECURITY_GROUP="default"
INSTANCE_NAME="gitforgits-automated-instance"

# Create the instance
openstack server create --flavor $FLAVOR --image $IMAGE_ID --
network $NETWORK_ID --key-name $KEY_NAME --security-group
$SECURITY_GROUP $INSTANCE_NAME

# Check the instance status
openstack server list | grep $INSTANCE_NAME
```

After creating the script, we need to make it executable:

```
chmod +x deploy_instance.sh
```

After this, we then execute the script to deploy the instance:

```
./deploy_instance.sh
```

The script will automatically create a new instance with the specified parameters, like how we manually deployed instances in previous recipes. The instance name will be **gitforgits-automated-instance**, and the script will output the instance's status once it is created.

Automating Deployment of Multiple Instances

In many scenarios, we may need to deploy multiple instances simultaneously. Automating this process can be done by extending the script to loop through the deployment process for several instances.

So here, we will modify the existing script to deploy multiple instances:

```
#!/bin/bash

# Variables
IMAGE_ID="<image_id>"
FLAVOR="m1.small"
NETWORK_ID="<network_id>"
KEY_NAME="gitforgits-key"
SECURITY_GROUP="default"
INSTANCE_COUNT=5  # Number of instances to deploy
BASE_INSTANCE_NAME="gitforgits-automated-instance"

# Loop to create multiple instances
for i in $(seq 1 $INSTANCE_COUNT); do
    INSTANCE_NAME="${BASE_INSTANCE_NAME}-${i}"
    openstack server create --flavor $FLAVOR --image $IMAGE_ID
--network $NETWORK_ID --key-name $KEY_NAME --security-group
$SECURITY_GROUP $INSTANCE_NAME
done

# Check the status of all instances
openstack server list | grep $BASE_INSTANCE_NAME
```

In the above script, the **INSTANCE_COUNT** is the number of instances we want to deploy. The script loops through the deployment process, creating instances named **gitforgits-automated-instance-1**, **gitforgits-automated-instance-2**, and so on.

Then, we will proceed to execute the script to deploy multiple instances:

```
./deploy_instance.sh
```

This will create the specified number of instances, each with its unique name. The script will then list all the deployed instances to verify their status.

Automating Post-Deployment Tasks

There are also post-deployment tasks that can be automated, like associating floating IPs, configuring security groups, and injecting metadata or configuration scripts.

Adding Floating IP Assignment

We can modify the script to automatically assign floating IPs to the instances:

```
# Assign a floating IP to each instance
for i in $(seq 1 $INSTANCE_COUNT); do
    INSTANCE_NAME="${BASE_INSTANCE_NAME}-${i}"
    FLOATING_IP=$(openstack floating ip create public -f value
-c floating_ip_address)
    openstack server add floating ip $INSTANCE_NAME
$FLOATING_IP
    echo "Assigned Floating IP $FLOATING_IP to $INSTANCE_NAME"
done
```

This section of the script creates a new floating IP from the public network and associates it with each instance.

Automating Security Group Rules

If specific security group rules are required for these instances, they can be added automatically as part of the deployment script:

```
# Add custom security group rules
openstack security group rule create --protocol tcp --dst-port
22 --ingress --description "Allow SSH" $SECURITY_GROUP
openstack security group rule create --protocol tcp --dst-port
80 --ingress --description "Allow HTTP" $SECURITY_GROUP
```

This ensures that each instance is correctly configured with the necessary security rules upon deployment.

Injecting Metadata

If we need to run specific configuration tasks on each instance after it launches, we can use Cloud-Init to inject scripts or metadata:

```
USER_DATA_FILE="user_data.sh"  # Path to the Cloud-Init script
```

```
openstack server create --flavor $FLAVOR --image $IMAGE_ID --
network $NETWORK_ID --key-name $KEY_NAME --security-group
$SECURITY_GROUP --user-data $USER_DATA_FILE $INSTANCE_NAME
```

This will pass a Cloud-Init script during instance creation, and thereby it automates the configuration tasks such as software installation, updates, or custom setups.

Scaling Deployment with Nova CLI

For larger environments or specific use cases, the GitforGits may need to deploy dozens or even hundreds of instances. The Nova CLI allows us to efficiently scale deployments, either by adjusting the script or using batch processing.

For very large deployments, we can consider breaking the deployment into batches to avoid overloading the compute resources:

```
BATCH_SIZE=10  # Number of instances per batch


for batch in $(seq 1 $((INSTANCE_COUNT / BATCH_SIZE))); do
    for i in $(seq 1 $BATCH_SIZE); do
        INSTANCE_NAME="${BASE_INSTANCE_NAME}-batch${batch}-
instance${i}"
        openstack server create --flavor $FLAVOR --image
$IMAGE_ID --network $NETWORK_ID --key-name $KEY_NAME --
security-group $SECURITY_GROUP $INSTANCE_NAME &
    done
    wait  # Wait for the batch to complete before starting the
next
done
```

This above script deploys instances in batches, with each batch launching simultaneously. The **wait** command ensures that each batch completes before starting the next, preventing resource contention.

If we need to scale instances dynamically based on demand, we can integrate the deployment scripts with OpenStack's autoscaling features (like Heat or external orchestration tools). For example, we could set up an autoscaling group that triggers instance deployments based on CPU load or network traffic.

Monitoring and Managing Automated Deployments

Once the automation scripts are in place, we can then monitor the deployments and manage instances effectively.

Monitoring Instance Status

After the deployment, we can monitor the status of the instances using:

```
openstack server list | grep $BASE_INSTANCE_NAME
```

It checks the status of all instances deployed by the script, allowing us to verify that they are running as expected.

Handling Failures

If an instance fails to deploy, the script can be modified to handle such cases, such as retrying the deployment or logging the failure:

```
if [ $? -ne 0 ]; then
    echo "Failed to deploy $INSTANCE_NAME. Retrying..."
    # Retry logic here
fi
```

This ensures that the deployment process is robust and can recover from errors.

Automating Cleanup

If instances are no longer needed, we can automate their cleanup with a simple script:

```
for i in $(seq 1 $INSTANCE_COUNT); do
    INSTANCE_NAME="${BASE_INSTANCE_NAME}-${i}"
    openstack server delete $INSTANCE_NAME
    echo "Deleted $INSTANCE_NAME"
done
```

This script automates the deletion of all instances created by the previous script, ensuring that resources are freed up when no longer needed.

Overall, in this recipe, we created scripts to automate single and multiple instance deployments, incorporating post-deployment tasks such as floating IP assignment, security group configuration, and Cloud-Init script injection. Additionally, we explored batch processing for large-scale deployments and integrated automation with monitoring and error handling.

Summary

To sum up, we mastered the art of optimizing and managing compute resources in Nova. At first, we looked at the process of manually deploying instances and the advantages of using SSH key injection to ensure secure access. We then learned to manage instance placement and affinity rules, which allow us to control where instances are deployed in the cloud.

The chapter goes deeper into Nova hypervisors, particularly KVM and QEMU for operating virtual machines in OpenStack. We learned to set up these hypervisors in the Nova environment for maximum efficiency and performance. Furthermore, we investigated configuring resource quotas and limits in Nova for managing resource allocation across multiple projects in GitforGits. Regarding automation, we learned to use Nova CLI to automate instance deployment, including scripting single and multiple instance deployments, as well as implementing post-deployment tasks such as assigning floating IP addresses and configuring security groups.

Chapter 6: Block Storage with Cinder

Introduction

The purpose of this chapter is to get us skilled with Cinder, OpenStack's block storage service, and to manage it. It teaches us to effectively manage and secure storage resources in an OpenStack environment. We will look at managing volume snapshots, which are an important feature for data protection and recovery. If something were to go wrong with the data, we could quickly restore it from a snapshot because they record the volume's condition at a specific moment in time. The chapter also discusses using Cinder for backup and restore operations so that the critical data can be securely stored and retrieved as needed.

As we progress, we will learn to configure Cinder to use various storage backends, such as LVM and Ceph, to optimize the storage infrastructure's performance, scalability, and redundancy. Another critical aspect we'll cover is automation, with a focus on using the Cinder CLI to automate volume management, streamline repetitive tasks, and increase efficiency. Finally, the chapter covers advanced topics such as creating bootable volumes for persistent instances and using volume encryption to protect sensitive data.

Recipe 1: Creating and Attaching Volumes to Instances

Storage blocks provide persistent storage that can be attached to instances, enabling them to store data beyond their lifecycle. It's Cinder that handles managing block storage. When we create and attach volumes, we make sure that the instances have the storage they need for applications, databases, and other important data. This recipe will walk us through creating and attaching volumes to the instances used by GitforGits, focusing on handling complex storage needs, like multiple volumes or large capacity volumes.

Creating Volume in Cinder

Before creating a volume, it's important to understand the storage requirements of the application. This includes the size of the volume, the type of storage backend (e.g., SSD, HDD), and any performance considerations.

For this example, we will create a 100 GB volume for a database application that requires high performance.

```
openstack volume create --size 100 --description "Database
Volume for GitforGits" gitforgits-db-volume
```

We can verify the creation of the volume by listing all volumes:

```
openstack volume list
```

The output should show the newly created volume with its status as **available**.

If the instance requires multiple volumes, we can repeat the process to create additional volumes. For example, we can create a 50 GB volume for log storage:

```
openstack volume create --size 50 --description "Log Volume
for GitforGits" gitforgits-log-volume
```

Attaching Volumes to Instance

Once the volumes are created, the next step is to attach them to an instance. For this example, let's attach the **gitforgits-db-volume** and **gitforgits-log-volume** to an instance that we previously deployed.

- Identify Instance

```
openstack server list
```

Note the **ID** or **Name** of the instance to which the volumes will be attached.

- Attach Database Volume

```
openstack server add volume <instance_id_or_name> gitforgits-
db-volume
```

It attaches the **gitforgits-db-volume** to the specified instance. You can verify the attachment by checking the instance details:

```
openstack server show <instance_id_or_name>
```

Here, we need to look for the **os-extended-volumes:volumes_attached** attribute to confirm that the volume is attached.

- Attach Log Volume

```
openstack server add volume <instance_id_or_name> gitforgits-
log-volume
```

This will attach the **gitforgits-log-volume** to the same instance. Again, we need to verify the attachment by reviewing the instance details.

Verifying Attached Volumes

After attaching the volumes, we should verify that they are recognized by the instance and are ready for use.

- Access Instance

```
ssh -i ~/.ssh/gitforgits-key ubuntu@<instance_ip>
```

- List Attached Disks

```
lsblk
```

Here, the output should display the newly attached volumes as block devices, such as **/dev/vdb** and **/dev/vdc**. These devices correspond to the **gitforgits-db-volume** and **gitforgits-log-volume**.

- Format Volumes

```
sudo mkfs.ext4 /dev/vdb
sudo mkfs.ext4 /dev/vdc
sudo mkdir /mnt/dbdata
sudo mkdir /mnt/logdata
```

It formats the volumes with the ext4 filesystem and creates directories where the volumes will be mounted.

- Mount Volumes

```
sudo mount /dev/vdb /mnt/dbdata
sudo mount /dev/vdc /mnt/logdata
```

It mounts the gitforgits-db-volume to /mnt/dbdata and the gitforgits-log-volume to /mnt/logdata.

Then, we will check the mounted filesystems to confirm:

```
df -h
```

The output should show the volumes mounted at **/mnt/dbdata** and **/mnt/logdata**, with their respective capacities.

Automating Volume Management

To automate the attachment and management of volumes in future deployments, we can use the

cloud-init scripts which will automate the process of attaching and configuring volumes during instance boot:

```
#!/bin/bash
mkfs.ext4 /dev/vdb
mkfs.ext4 /dev/vdc
mkdir /mnt/dbdata
mkdir /mnt/logdata
mount /dev/vdb /mnt/dbdata
mount /dev/vdc /mnt/logdata
```

We then pass this script to the instance during creation using the **--user-data** option:

```
openstack server create --flavor m1.small --image <image_id> --network <network_id> --key-name gitforgits-key --security-group default --user-data myscript.sh gitforgits-automated-instance
```

This automates the volume management process. This whole recipe or the process provides persistent storage to the instances, and thereby to handle data-intensive tasks and applications effectively.

Recipe 2: Managing Volume Snapshots for Data Protection

The Cinder's volume snapshots are a game-changer. They let us capture the state of a volume at a specific point in time, which is super important for data protection. This feature lets us recover quickly from accidental deletions, data corruption, or other unexpected issues. They let you back up your data without taking the volume offline. In this recipe, we're going to create, manage, and use snapshots for the volumes we've made and attached to instances so far.

Creating Volume Snapshot

Before creating a snapshot, identify the volume we wish to snapshot. So here, we will create a snapshot of the **gitforgits-db-volume** we created in the previous recipe.

For this, we will first list the available volumes to confirm the volume name or ID:

```
openstack volume list
```

It lists all the volumes, allowing us to identify the correct one for snapshotting.

We will now create a snapshot of the volume:

```
openstack volume snapshot create --volume gitforgits-db-volume
--name gitforgits-db-snapshot --description "Snapshot of
GitforGits DB Volume"
```

In the above script,

- **--volume gitforgits-db-volume** specifies the volume for which the snapshot will be created.
- **--name gitforgits-db-snapshot** provides a name for the snapshot. And,
- **--description** adds a description for the snapshot.

It then creates a snapshot named **gitforgits-db-snapshot** of the **gitforgits-db-volume**. We can monitor the creation process by listing the snapshots:

```
openstack volume snapshot list
```

The status should initially show as **creating** and change to **available** once the snapshot is completed.

Managing Volume Snapshots

Once we have created a snapshot, managing it becomes a need for maintaining an organized and efficient storage environment. This involves viewing, deleting, and restoring from snapshots as needed.

So, to view detailed information about a specific snapshot, we use:

```
openstack volume snapshot show gitforgits-db-snapshot
```

It displays detailed information about the snapshot, including its size, creation date, and status. It helps us verify that the snapshot was created correctly and is ready for use.

If a snapshot is no longer needed, we can delete it to free up storage space:

```
openstack volume snapshot delete gitforgits-db-snapshot
```

It deletes the **gitforgits-db-snapshot**, permanently removing the snapshot from the storage system.

In addition, one of the primary uses of snapshots is to restore a volume to a previous state. Now, to restore a volume from a snapshot, we can either create a new volume from the snapshot or replace the existing volume with the snapshot data.

So here, to create a new volume from the snapshot:

```
openstack volume create --snapshot gitforgits-db-snapshot --
size 100 --description "Restored DB Volume" gitforgits-db-
restored-volume
```

This then creates a new volume named **gitforgits-db-restored-volume**, identical to the original volume at the time of the snapshot.

If we need to revert the original volume to the snapshot state, we will need to delete the original volume and recreate it from the snapshot:

```
openstack volume delete gitforgits-db-volume
```

Then, create a new volume from the snapshot using the same name:

```
openstack volume create --snapshot gitforgits-db-snapshot --
size 100 --description "Restored DB Volume" gitforgits-db-
volume
```

This process restores the volume to its state at the time of the snapshot, effectively reverting any changes made since the snapshot was taken.

Automating Snapshot Management

In environments where volumes are frequently updated or critical data is involved, we can automate the snapshot management for regular backups without manual intervention. We can schedule regular snapshot creation using cron jobs or other automation tools.

Following is a simple cron job that creates a snapshot of the **gitforgits-db-volume** every day at midnight:

Here, we will first open the crontab for editing:

```
crontab -e
```

And then, we will add the following line to schedule the snapshot creation:

```
0 0 * * * openstack volume snapshot create --volume
gitforgits-db-volume --name gitforgits-db-snapshot-$(date
+\%Y\%m\%d) --description "Daily Snapshot of GitforGits DB
Volume"
```

Here, the cron job will create a snapshot with a timestamp in its name to identify the date of each snapshot.

Now, to prevent the accumulation of too many snapshots, which can consume significant storage space, we can automate the deletion of older snapshots. For example, to delete snapshots older than 7 days, we can add another cron job:

```
0 1 * * * openstack volume snapshot list --format value --
column ID --column Created_at | awk -v d=$(date -d "7 days
ago" +\%Y-\%m-\%d) '$2 < d {print $1}' | xargs -I {} openstack
volume snapshot delete {}
```

This job runs daily at 1 AM and deletes snapshots older than 7 days. It ensures that the storage usage remains under control.

Recipe 3: Cinder for Backup and Restore Operations

In addition to snapshots, the Cinder provides robust backup and restore functionality for protecting data against failures, corruption, or accidental deletions. Unlike snapshots, which are typically stored locally and capture the state of a volume at a specific point in time, backups are usually stored externally, offering an extra layer of protection. In this recipe, we'll practice to perform backup and restore operations on the volumes we previously created for GitforGits.

Creating Volume Backup

Before creating a backup, we need to identify the volume we wish to back up. For example, we can create a backup of the **gitforgits-db-volume** that we worked with earlier.

For this, we will list the available volumes to confirm the volume name or ID:

```
openstack volume list
```

It lists all the volumes, allowing us to identify the correct one for backup. Now, to create a backup of the volume, we can then use the following:

```
openstack volume backup create --name gitforgits-db-backup --
description "Backup of GitforGits DB Volume" gitforgits-db-
volume
```

It creates a backup named **gitforgits-db-backup** for the **gitforgits-db-volume**.

After this, we can then monitor the backup creation process by listing the backups:

```
openstack volume backup list
```

The status should initially show as **`creating`** and change to **`available`** once the backup is completed.

Managing Volume Backups

Once the backup is created, we can manage it, including viewing details, deleting, or restoring from the backup.

So here, to view detailed information about a specific backup, we can use:

```
openstack volume backup show gitforgits-db-backup
```

It displays detailed information about the backup, including its size, creation date, and status. It helps us verify that the backup was created correctly and is ready for use.

If a backup is no longer needed, we can delete it to free up storage space:

```
openstack volume backup delete gitforgits-db-backup
```

It deletes the **`gitforgits-db-backup`**, permanently removing the backup from the storage system. Be sure that the backup is no longer needed before deletion, as this process cannot be undone.

Restoring Volume from Backup

The primary purpose of creating backups is to restore data when needed. The Cinder makes it easy to restore a volume from a backup, either by creating a new volume from the backup or by overwriting an existing volume.

So, to restore a volume from a backup and create a new volume, we can do it using:

```
openstack volume create --backup gitforgits-db-backup --size
100 --description "Restored DB Volume from Backup" gitforgits-
db-restored-from-backup
```

If we need to restore the original volume from the backup, we will first need to delete the existing volume and then restore it from the backup.

```
openstack volume delete gitforgits-db-volume
```

Then, we can create a new volume from the backup using the same name:

```
openstack volume create --backup gitforgits-db-backup --size
100 --description "Restored DB Volume from Backup" gitforgits-
db-volume
```

This effectively restores the **gitforgits-db-volume** to its state at the time of the backup to recover the data if the original volume was corrupted or lost.

Automating Backup Management

Like snapshots, we can schedule regular backups using cron jobs or other automation tools. Following is a quick cron job that creates a backup of the **gitforgits-db-volume** every week:

```
crontab -e
```

Here, we will add the following line to schedule the weekly backup:

```
0 2 * * 0 openstack volume backup create --name gitforgits-db-backup-$(date +\%Y\%m\%d) --description "Weekly Backup of GitforGits DB Volume" gitforgits-db-volume
```

This cron job creates a new backup every Sunday at 2 AM, naming each backup with the date it was created.

But, if we want to prevent backups from consuming excessive storage, automate the deletion of older backups:

```
0 3 * * 0 openstack volume backup list --format value --column ID --column Created_at | awk -v d=$(date -d "4 weeks ago" +\%Y-\%m-\%d) '$2 < d {print $1}' | xargs -I {} openstack volume backup delete {}
```

This job runs every Sunday at 3 AM and deletes backups older than 4 weeks, ensuring that only recent backups are retained.

Recipe 4: Configuring Cinder to use Storage Backend

Cinder, the block storage service, is designed to work with a variety of storage backends, allowing administrators to optimize storage resources based on performance, scalability, and cost requirements. For GitforGits, we have previously chosen Ceph to be the preferred storage backend due to its scalability and reliability. In this recipe, we will learn to configure Cinder to use Ceph as the storage backend.

Preparing Ceph Cluster

Before configuring Cinder, we will confirm that the Ceph cluster is properly set up and operational, like having the Ceph monitor nodes, OSDs (Object Storage Daemons), and the Ceph client installed on the Cinder node.

```
ceph status
```

The output should indicate a healthy cluster with all OSDs up and running. Then, on the Cinder node, we will install the Ceph client packages:

```
sudo apt-get install ceph ceph-common
```

After this, the Cinder node can communicate with the Ceph cluster.

Configuring Cinder for Ceph

Now that the Ceph cluster is ready, we can configure Cinder to use it as the storage backend. For this, we will access the Cinder configuration file **cinder.conf** on the Cinder node:

```
sudo nano /etc/cinder/cinder.conf
```

Then, we will add or update the following sections to configure Ceph as the storage backend:

```
[DEFAULT]
enabled_backends = ceph

[ceph]
volume_driver = cinder.volume.drivers.rbd.RBDDriver
rbd_pool = volumes
rbd_ceph_conf = /etc/ceph/ceph.conf
rbd_user = cinder
rbd_secret_uuid = <uuid_of_the_ceph_secret>
volume_backend_name = ceph
```

In the above script,

- **enabled_backends = ceph** specifies that Ceph is the enabled backend.
- **volume_driver** sets the driver to **RBDDriver** for Ceph's RADOS Block Device (RBD).
- **rbd_pool = volumes** specifies the Ceph pool used for Cinder volumes.
- **rbd_ceph_conf = /etc/ceph/ceph.conf** points to the Ceph configuration

file.

- **rbd_user = cinder** specifies the Ceph user for Cinder.
- **rbd_secret_uuid = <uuid_of_the_ceph_secret>** references the secret UUID for authentication. And,
- **volume_backend_name = ceph** names the backend, used when configuring multiple backends.

After this, on the Ceph monitor node, we will now create a Ceph user for Cinder:

```
ceph auth get-or-create client.cinder mon 'allow r' osd 'allow
class-read object_prefix rbd_children, allow rwx pool=volumes'
```

It creates a user **client.cinder** with permissions to read and write to the **volumes** pool.

The next step is to generate a UUID for the secret key:

```
uuidgen
```

Now here, the UUID, as it will be used in the Cinder configuration. On the Ceph monitor node, we will generate the key for the **cinder** user:

```
ceph auth get-key client.cinder | sudo tee
/etc/ceph/client.cinder.keyring
```

After this, we will create a secret in OpenStack to store the key:

```
sudo virsh secret-define --file
/etc/ceph/client.cinder.keyring

sudo virsh secret-set-value --secret <uuid_of_the_ceph_secret>
--base64 $(ceph auth get-key client.cinder)
```

Here, we need to replace **<uuid_of_the_ceph_secret>** with the UUID generated earlier. After updating the configuration, we can then restart the Cinder services to apply the changes:

```
sudo systemctl restart cinder-volume

sudo systemctl restart cinder-scheduler
```

This will confirm that the Cinder is now using Ceph as its storage backend.

With this, we learned to configure Cinder to use a specific storage backend, focusing on setting up Ceph. We covered the necessary steps to integrate Cinder with Ceph, from configuring the Cinder service to creating and verifying volumes in the Ceph cluster.

Recipe 5: Automating Volume Management with Cinder CLI

While manual management of volumes is feasible in smaller setups, automation becomes essential as the environment grows. The Cinder CLI offers powerful commands for administrators to automate various volume management tasks, such as creating, attaching, detaching, and deleting volumes. In this recipe, we'll learn to the Cinder CLI to automate these tasks, and will aim for improving efficiency and reducing the potential for human error.

Automate Volume Creation

The automation of volume creation saves time, especially when provisioning multiple volumes for different instances or projects. So here, we will start by creating a simple shell script to automate the creation of multiple volumes.

```
nano create_volumes.sh
#!/bin/bash

# Variables
VOLUME_SIZE=50  # Size of each volume in GB
VOLUME_COUNT=5  # Number of volumes to create
BASE_VOLUME_NAME="gitforgits-volume"

# Loop to create multiple volumes
for i in $(seq 1 $VOLUME_COUNT); do
    VOLUME_NAME="${BASE_VOLUME_NAME}-${i}"
    openstack volume create --size $VOLUME_SIZE --description
"Automated Volume $i for GitforGits" $VOLUME_NAME
    echo "Created volume $VOLUME_NAME"
done
```

This script creates five volumes, each 50 GB in size, with names like **`gitforgits-volume-1`**, **`gitforgits-volume-2`**, and so on.

After saving the script, we will make it executable and execute accordingly:

```
chmod +x create_volumes.sh
./create_volumes.sh
```

The script will automatically create the specified number of volumes and display their creation status.

Automating Volume Attachment

There are also post-deployment tasks that can be automated, like associating floating IPs, configuring security groups, and injecting metadata or configuration scripts.

```
nano attach_volumes.sh
#!/bin/bash

# Variables
INSTANCE_ID="<instance_id>"  # Replace with the actual
instance ID
BASE_VOLUME_NAME="gitforgits-volume"
VOLUME_COUNT=5  # Number of volumes to attach

# Loop to attach each volume to the instance
for i in $(seq 1 $VOLUME_COUNT); do
    VOLUME_NAME="${BASE_VOLUME_NAME}-${i}"
    openstack server add volume $INSTANCE_ID $VOLUME_NAME
    echo "Attached $VOLUME_NAME to instance $INSTANCE_ID"
done
chmod +x attach_volumes.sh
./attach_volumes.sh
```

The script will attach each volume to the instance, displaying the status of each operation.

Automating Volume Detachment and Deletion

The volume detachment and deletion are equally important tasks that can also be automated to ensure that unused resources are freed up promptly. So here, we will automate the detachment of volumes from an instance using the following script:

```
nano detach_volumes.sh
#!/bin/bash

# Variables
INSTANCE_ID="<instance_id>"  # Replace with the actual
instance ID
BASE_VOLUME_NAME="gitforgits-volume"
VOLUME_COUNT=5  # Number of volumes to detach

# Loop to detach each volume from the instance
for i in $(seq 1 $VOLUME_COUNT); do
    VOLUME_NAME="${BASE_VOLUME_NAME}-${i}"
    openstack server remove volume $INSTANCE_ID $VOLUME_NAME
    echo "Detached $VOLUME_NAME from instance $INSTANCE_ID"
done
./detach_volumes.sh
```

The script will detach each volume from the instance. After detaching volumes, we can automate their deletion with another script:

```
nano delete_volumes.sh
#!/bin/bash

# Variables
BASE_VOLUME_NAME="gitforgits-volume"
VOLUME_COUNT=5  # Number of volumes to delete

# Loop to delete each volume
for i in $(seq 1 $VOLUME_COUNT); do
    VOLUME_NAME="${BASE_VOLUME_NAME}-${i}"
```

```
    openstack volume delete $VOLUME_NAME
    echo "Deleted volume $VOLUME_NAME"
done
```

This script will delete each of the specified volumes.

Scheduling Automated Tasks

To fully automate volume management tasks, consider scheduling these scripts to run at specific intervals using cron jobs. Here, to schedule the creation of volumes every Monday at midnight, we will add the following to the crontab:

```
crontab -e
0 0 * * 1 /path/to/create_volumes.sh
```

The script then runs automatically at the specified time. Also, to delete volumes automatically every Sunday at midnight:

```
0 0 * * 0 /path/to/delete_volumes.sh
```

This keeps the storage usage optimized by regularly removing unneeded volumes.

With this, we demonstrated to automate various volume management tasks using the Cinder CLI. And, we covered the automation of volume creation, attachment, detachment, and deletion, providing practical examples that can be adapted to the needs of GitforGits. Additionally, we learned to schedule these tasks using cron jobs with minimal manual intervention.

Recipe 6: Implementing Volume Encryption for Data Security

Setting up Encryption Key Manager

Before we can implement volume encryption in Cinder, we need to have an encryption key manager configured. The OpenStack typically uses Barbican to handle encryption keys.

If Barbican is not already installed, we can install it:

```
sudo apt-get update
sudo apt-get install barbican-api barbican-keystone-listener barbican-worker barbican-common
```

After installation, we then configure Barbican by editing **barbican.conf** file:

```
sudo nano /etc/barbican/barbican.conf
```

Now here, we must confirm that the key manager section is configured correctly:

```
[keystone_authtoken]
auth_uri = http://<keystone-host>:5000
memcached_servers = <keystone-host>:11211
auth_type = password
project_domain_name = Default
user_domain_name = Default
project_name = service
username = barbican
password = <barbican-password>
```

After this, we then restart the Barbican services to apply the changes:

```
sudo systemctl restart barbican-api barbican-worker barbican-keystone-listener
```

Now that Barbican is set up, we can create an encryption type that will be applied to the volumes.

Creating Encryption Type for Volumes

We will now create an encryption type for the volume type you're using. For this, we will first list the existing volume types to choose the appropriate one:

```
openstack volume type list
```

Next, we then create an encryption type for the desired volume type:

```
openstack volume type create --encryption-provider luks --name gitforgits-encrypted-volumes
```

It creates a new volume type called **gitforgits-encrypted-volumes** with LUKS (Linux Unified Key Setup) as the encryption provider.

Here, we can specify additional encryption details, such as cipher and key size, when creating the encryption type:

```
openstack volume type encryption set --provider luks --cipher
aes-xts-plain64 --key-size 256 --control-location front-end
gitforgits-encrypted-volumes
```

It configures the encryption to use the AES cipher with a 256-bit key.

Creating and Attaching Encrypted Volumes

With the encryption type configured, we can now create and attach encrypted volumes to the instances.

The following will create a new encrypted volume:

```
openstack volume create --type gitforgits-encrypted-volumes --
size 100 --description "Encrypted Database Volume" gitforgits-
encrypted-db-volume
```

It creates a 100 GB encrypted volume named **gitforgits-encrypted-db-volume**.

After this, we then attach the newly created encrypted volume to an instance:

```
openstack server add volume <instance_id_or_name> gitforgits-
encrypted-db-volume
```

This attaches the encrypted volume to the specified instance, ready for use.

Verifying Volume Encryption

After creating and attaching the encrypted volume, we will verify that the encryption is active. For this, we will access the instance where the encrypted volume is attached:

```
ssh -i ~/.ssh/gitforgits-key ubuntu@<instance_ip>
```

next, we then list the block devices to verify that the encrypted volume is recognized:

```
lsblk
```

The output should show the encrypted volume as a block device, typically with the name **/dev/dm-0** or similar.

Now here, to ensure that the volume is encrypted, we can check the encryption details using the following:

```
sudo cryptsetup status <device_name>
```

Replace **<device_name>** with the name of the encrypted block device (e.g., **/dev/dm-0**). The output should confirm that the device is encrypted with the specified cipher and key size.

Automating Creation of Encrypted Volumes

To streamline the deployment of encrypted volumes, we can automate their creation using a script as below:

```
nano create_encrypted_volumes.sh
#!/bin/bash


# Variables
VOLUME_SIZE=50  # Size of each volume in GB
VOLUME_COUNT=3  # Number of volumes to create
VOLUME_TYPE="gitforgits-encrypted-volumes"
BASE_VOLUME_NAME="gitforgits-encrypted-volume"


# Loop to create multiple encrypted volumes
for i in $(seq 1 $VOLUME_COUNT); do
    VOLUME_NAME="${BASE_VOLUME_NAME}-${i}"
    openstack volume create --type $VOLUME_TYPE --size
$VOLUME_SIZE --description "Automated Encrypted Volume $i for
GitforGits" $VOLUME_NAME
    echo "Created encrypted volume $VOLUME_NAME"
done
```

This script creates three 50 GB encrypted volumes.

To sum up, we learned to implement volume encryption using the Barbican key manager and Cinder CLI. We practiced to configure encryption for volumes, create encrypted volumes, attach them to instances, and verify the encryption status. Additionally, we automated the creation of encrypted volumes to secure its data effectively and efficiently in the cloud environment.

Summary

To summarize, this chapter focused on managing block storage with Cinder. The chapter began by going over the process of creating and attaching volumes to instances, which allowed for persistent storage that could be used by the virtual machines deployed in the environment. This was followed by learning how to manage volume snapshots, which are critical for data protection because they capture the volume's state at a specific point in time and provide a method for quick restoration if necessary. The chapter also covered backup and restore operations, followed by a deeper layer of data protection to ensure that data is securely backed up and restored from external storage. A significant portion of the chapter was dedicated to configuring Cinder to use various storage backends, with a particular emphasis on integrating Ceph as the storage backend for GitforGits. This included installing Ceph, configuring Cinder to work with it, and ensuring that the storage infrastructure was optimized for performance and scalability.

Later, we moved on to automation, which involved automating volume management tasks with Cinder CLI such as automating volume creation, attachment, detachment, and deletion, streamlining operations, and minimizing manual effort. Finally, the chapter covered implementing volume encryption to secure data at rest which included configuring encryption types, creating encrypted volumes, and verifying the encryption status. All these lessons together provided an in-depth view of how to effectively manage, secure, and automate block storage in an OpenStack environment.

Chapter 7: Load Balancing with Octavia

Introduction

In this chapter, we're going to learn to use Octavia to set up and administer load balancing in an OpenStack environment. This chapter will teach to set up and manage load balancers to make cloud-based applications more reliable and perform better.

It starts by installing and configuring Octavia, and then we'll learn to create and manage load balancer pools to distribute incoming requests to backend servers. Then, the chapter moves on to configuring load balancer listeners and virtual IP addresses (VIPs). Plus, you'll dive into SSL termination, which keeps traffic between clients and the load balancer safe by handling SSL processing. Finally, the chapter talks about integrating Octavia with Neutron networking to make sure everything works smoothly together in the OpenStack cloud. Once you're done with this chapter, you'll have a clear understanding of how to implement and manage load balancing to improve the availability and resilience of the applications.

Recipe 1: Installing and Configuring Octavia

Load Balancer as a Service (LBaaS) and Octavia

For cloud computing, keeping apps available and responsive is key. LBaaS is a key feature that helps achieve this by distributing incoming network traffic across multiple servers. It is great because it makes sure no single server is overloaded, and this thing improves the performance and availability of applications. With OpenStack, Octavia is the go-to LBaaS solution, made to fit in perfectly with the rest of the OpenStack ecosystem.

What is LBaaS?

LBaaS allows cloud administrators and users to deploy load balancers without worrying about the underlying infrastructure. It automates the process of distributing network traffic to multiple backend servers, ensuring efficient resource usage and high availability. It is particularly useful in environments where applications need to scale dynamically in response to varying workloads.

Introducing Octavia

Octavia is the official OpenStack service designed to provide LBaaS functionality. It is an advanced and highly scalable load balancing solution that operates by managing a fleet of virtual machines, known as amphorae, which act as load balancers. Octavia's design is based on the concept of a "controller-worker" architecture, where the Octavia controller manages and orchestrates the creation, configuration, and maintenance of the amphorae, while the amphorae themselves handle the actual load balancing tasks. It supports a wide range of load balancing algorithms and features, including SSL termination, L7 content switching, and health monitoring.

In this recipe, we will install and configure Octavia to enable LBaaS in the OpenStack environment.

Preparing Environment for Octavia

Before installing Octavia, the OpenStack environment should be running fine with the necessary components like Neutron and Keystone. And both these are already taught in chapter 2 and chapter 4.

We proceed then, On the controller node, we will install the necessary dependencies for Octavia:

```
sudo apt-get update
sudo apt-get install -y octavia-api octavia-health-manager octavia-housekeeping octavia-worker python3-octaviaclient
```

Next, we will create a user for Octavia in Keystone:

```
openstack user create --domain default --password <password> octavia
openstack role add --project service --user octavia admin
```

It creates the **`octavia`** user and grants the necessary roles.

Next, we then register the Octavia service in Keystone:

```
openstack service create --name octavia --description "OpenStack Load Balancing" load-balancer
```

After this, we then create the API endpoints for Octavia:

```
openstack endpoint create --region RegionOne load-balancer public http://<controller_ip>:9876
openstack endpoint create --region RegionOne load-balancer internal http://<controller_ip>:9876
openstack endpoint create --region RegionOne load-balancer admin http://<controller_ip>:9876
```

It registers the Octavia service endpoints in Keystone, and thereby allows it to be accessed by other OpenStack components.

Configuring Octavia

After the initial setup, we will configure the Octavia to integrate with the rest of the OpenStack environment.

Configuring Octavia API

So here, we will edit the **octavia.conf**:

```
sudo nano /etc/octavia/octavia.conf
```

In the **[DEFAULT]** section, we will configure the basics:

```
[DEFAULT]
transport_url =
rabbit://openstack:<RABBITMQ_PASSWORD>@<controller_ip>
auth_strategy = keystone
```

In the **[keystone_authtoken]** section, we then configure Keystone authentication:

```
[keystone_authtoken]
www_authenticate_uri = http://<controller_ip>:5000
auth_url = http://<controller_ip>:5000
memcached_servers = <controller_ip>:11211
auth_type = password
project_domain_name = Default
user_domain_name = Default
project_name = service
username = octavia
password = <password>
```

In the **[controller_worker]** section, we will configure the amphora image:

```
[controller_worker]
amp_image_tag = <amphora_image_tag>
amp_flavor_id = <flavor_id>
amp_boot_network_list = <network_id>
```

Configuring Amphora Image

The Octavia uses amphorae, which are virtual machines running HAProxy, to perform load balancing. So here, we now create and upload an amphora image:

```
wget https://tarballs.openstack.org/octavia/test-images/test-only-amphora-x64-haproxy.qcow2

openstack image create "amphora-x64-haproxy" --file test-only-amphora-x64-haproxy.qcow2 --disk-format qcow2 --container-format bare --tag amphora
```

It uploads the amphora image to Glance and tags it appropriately.

Once the configuration is complete, we then restart the Octavia services to apply the changes:

```
sudo systemctl restart octavia-worker

sudo systemctl restart octavia-health-manager

sudo systemctl restart octavia-housekeeping

sudo systemctl restart octavia-api
```

Verifying Octavia

Finally, we will verify that Octavia has been successfully installed and configured.

```
sudo systemctl status octavia-worker octavia-health-manager octavia-housekeeping octavia-api

openstack loadbalancer list
```

All services should show as active and running. Since we haven't created any load balancers yet, it should return an empty list. However, it confirms that Octavia is correctly integrated with OpenStack.

Recipe 2: Creating and Managing Load Balancer Pools

In Octavia, a load balancer pool is a logical set of servers that share the incoming traffic. The load balancer distributes incoming requests across the members of the pool based on the selected load balancing algorithm. In this recipe, we'll create load balancers, and then we'll practice to manage these pools under different scenarios.

Creating Load Balancer

The first step in setting up a load balancer is to create the load balancer itself, which will distribute traffic across the backend servers (pool members).

Create Load Balancer

The below one creates a new load balancer:

```
openstack loadbalancer create --name gitforgits-lb --vip-
subnet-id <subnet_id>
```

In the above,

- **--name gitforgits-lb** is the name of the load balancer. And,
- **--vip-subnet-id <subnet_id>** is the subnet ID where the VIP of the load balancer will be created.

This above command creates a load balancer named **gitforgits-lb** with a virtual IP in the specified subnet.

Check Load Balancer Status

After creating the load balancer, we then check its status:

```
openstack loadbalancer show gitforgits-lb
```

The status should initially show as **PENDING_CREATE** and then change to **ACTIVE** once the load balancer is ready.

Setting up and Managing Load Balancer Pools

We now move to set up the pool to distribute traffic among the backend servers.

Create Load Balancer Pool

Create a pool for the load balancer:

```
openstack loadbalancer pool create --name gitforgits-pool --
lb-algorithm ROUND_ROBIN --listener <listener_id> --protocol
HTTP
```

Here,

- **--name gitforgits-pool** is the name of the pool.
- **--lb-algorithm ROUND_ROBIN** is the load balancing algorithm to use (e.g., ROUND_ROBIN, LEAST_CONNECTIONS, SOURCE_IP).
- **--listener <listener_id>** is the ID of the listener that the pool will use. And,
- **--protocol HTTP** is the protocol used by the pool.

Add Members to Pool

After this, we then add members (backend servers) to the pool:

```
openstack loadbalancer member create --subnet-id <subnet_id> --address <server_ip> --protocol-port 80 gitforgits-pool
```

Here, we will repeat the above code line for each server we want to add to the pool:

```
openstack loadbalancer member create --subnet-id <subnet_id> --address 192.168.1.10 --protocol-port 80 gitforgits-pool

openstack loadbalancer member create --subnet-id <subnet_id> --address 192.168.1.11 --protocol-port 80 gitforgits-pool
```

This adds two members to the **gitforgits-pool**, with IP addresses **192.168.1.10** and **192.168.1.11**.

Check Pool Status

After adding members, we then check the status of the pool:

```
openstack loadbalancer pool show gitforgits-pool
```

The status should indicate that the pool is **ACTIVE** and list the members that were added.

Managing Load Balancer Pools

Scaling Pool

As traffic increases, we may need to scale the pool by adding more backend servers:

```
openstack loadbalancer member create --subnet-id <subnet_id> --address 192.168.1.12 --protocol-port 80 gitforgits-pool
```

It adds a new member to the pool, allowing the load balancer to distribute traffic across an additional server. If a server is underperforming or needs to be taken offline for maintenance, we can remove it from the pool:

```
openstack loadbalancer member delete gitforgits-pool <member_id>
```

It removes the specified member from the pool.

Changing Load Balancing Algorithm

Depending on the application's needs, we might need to change the load balancing algorithm:

```
openstack loadbalancer pool set --lb-algorithm
LEAST_CONNECTIONS gitforgits-pool
```

It changes the load balancing algorithm for **gitforgits-pool** to **LEAST_CONNECTIONS**, which directs traffic to the server with the fewest active connections.

Monitoring and Health Checking

Here, the health monitors can be added to ensure that traffic is only sent to healthy servers:

```
openstack loadbalancer healthmonitor create --delay 5 --
timeout 3 --max-retries 3 --type HTTP --pool gitforgits-pool -
-url-path /
```

In the above code,

- **--delay 5** is the time in seconds between health checks.
- **--timeout 3** is the time in seconds to wait for a response.
- **--max-retries 3** is the number of retries before marking a member as unhealthy.
- **--type HTTP** is the protocol used by the health monitor. And,
- **--url-path /** is the URL path to check.

It creates a health monitor that checks each member of **gitforgits-pool** every 5 seconds. If a member fails to respond three times in a row, it is marked as unhealthy and removed from the pool until it recovers.

After this, we then verify the health monitor status:

```
openstack loadbalancer healthmonitor show <healthmonitor_id>
```

It provides the status and configuration details of the health monitor.

Testing Load Balancer Functionality

We will now test the configuration to ensure everything is functioning as expected. For this, we will access the VIP of the load balancer to verify that traffic is correctly distributed among the pool members:

```
curl http://<vip_ip>
```

The response should indicate that the traffic is being handled by one of the backend servers. And, to test the robustness of the load balancer, we will simulate a failure by shutting down one of the backend servers:

```
sudo systemctl stop apache2
```

After this, we then access the VIP again to ensure that the load balancer routes traffic to the remaining healthy servers.

With such simple steps, we can easily create and manage the load balancer pools.

Recipe 3: Configuring Load Balancer Listeners and VIPs

Load Balancer Listeners and VIPs

The listeners and Virtual IPs (VIPs) are quite an essential component of a load balancer that determine how traffic is handled and routed to backend servers. While the load balancer itself is responsible for distributing traffic across pool members, listeners define how the load balancer listens for incoming connections, and VIPs serve as the endpoint for these connections.

A listener is generally configured on a specific protocol and port, and it is responsible for receiving incoming traffic on the load balancer. The listener defines the protocol (e.g., HTTP, HTTPS, TCP) and the port number on which the load balancer will accept traffic. Each listener is associated with a load balancer and directs traffic to the appropriate pool based on its configuration.

And, the VIP is the IP address that clients use to access the load balancer. When clients send traffic to the VIP, the load balancer's listener receives this traffic and processes it according to the configured rules and algorithms. The VIP is a key element because it abstracts the actual IP addresses of the backend servers, thus providing a single-entry point for accessing the load-balanced service.

In this recipe, we will configure listeners and VIPs for the load balancers. Here, we will walk through the steps to set up these components and ensure they are properly configured to handle incoming traffic.

Configuring Load Balancer Listener

The first step in handling traffic is to set up a listener that will receive incoming connections on a specific protocol and port.

Create Listener

The below one creates a listener for the **`gitforgits-lb`** load balancer:

```
openstack loadbalancer listener create --name gitforgits-http-
listener --protocol HTTP --protocol-port 80 --loadbalancer
gitforgits-lb
```

It creates an HTTP listener named **gitforgits-http-listener** that listens on port 80 for the **gitforgits-lb** load balancer.

Verify Listener Configuration

After creating the listener, we then verify its configuration:

```
openstack loadbalancer listener show gitforgits-http-listener
```

The output should display the details of the listener, including its protocol, port, and status. The status should be **ACTIVE** if the listener was successfully created.

Configuring VIP

The VIP is the address through which the load balancer is accessed by clients. This IP address is automatically assigned when the load balancer is created, but it's important to ensure it's configured correctly and associated with the correct listener.

So, to view the VIP assigned to the load balancer:

```
openstack loadbalancer show gitforgits-lb
```

Here, you need to look for the **vip_address** field in the output, which shows the IP address assigned to the load balancer. This is the address that clients will use to send traffic to the load balancer.

If we need to assign a specific static IP as the VIP instead of using the automatically assigned one, we can specify it when creating the load balancer:

```
openstack loadbalancer create --name gitforgits-lb --vip-
address <static_ip> --vip-subnet-id <subnet_id>
```

In the above, we need to replace **<static_ip>** with the desired static IP address and **<subnet_id>** with the ID of the subnet where the VIP will reside. It ensures that the load balancer uses a specific IP address as its VIP.

Managing Listeners and VIPs

We may need to update or manage listeners and VIPs to handle different traffic patterns or application requirements.

Update Listener

If we need to change the listener's configuration, such as its protocol or port, we can update it using the following:

```
openstack loadbalancer listener set --protocol HTTPS --
protocol-port 443 gitforgits-http-listener
```

It changes the protocol to HTTPS and the port to 443. You might use this if we need to switch from HTTP to HTTPS for secure communications.

Add New Listener to Same Load Balancer

We can also add multiple listeners to the same load balancer, each handling different protocols or ports.

```
openstack loadbalancer listener create --name gitforgits-
https-listener --protocol HTTPS --protocol-port 443 --
loadbalancer gitforgits-lb
```

The above one adds a second listener to the **`gitforgits-lb`** load balancer to handle both HTTP and HTTPS traffic.

Testing Configuration

After setting up the listeners and VIP, it's crucial to test the configuration to ensure that traffic is properly routed through the load balancer.

Access Load Balancer via VIP

Test access to the load balancer by using the VIP:

```
curl http://<vip_ip>
```

The response should indicate that the request has been routed through the load balancer and handled by one of the backend servers.

Test Different Protocols

If we have multiple listeners (e.g., HTTP and HTTPS), test each protocol by accessing the VIP with the appropriate protocol:

```
curl -k https://<vip_ip>
```

The **`-k`** flag is used to bypass SSL verification for testing purposes. It should return a response indicating that the HTTPS listener is correctly routing traffic.

So, for this recipe, we first set up listeners to handle traffic coming in on certain protocols and ports. Then, we made sure the VIP was assigned correctly and working properly. We also talked about how to manage and update listeners and VIPs, which makes it easier to handle different traffic needs.

Recipe 4: Using SSL Termination with Octavia

Basically, SSL termination is a process where the SSL encryption and decryption tasks are moved from the backend servers to the load balancer. So, incoming SSL-encrypted traffic is decrypted at the load balancer before being sent to the backend servers, and outgoing traffic is encrypted by the load balancer before being sent to the client.

When it comes to Octavia, we really need SSL termination to keep communication between clients and the load balancer secure. When we implement SSL termination, we can make sure that data is encrypted as it moves across the internet, adding an extra layer of security for the apps. It also makes certificate management easier because you only need the certificates on the load balancer, not on each backend server.

Preparing SSL Certificates

Before configuring SSL termination, we need to have SSL certificates ready. These certificates will be used by the load balancer to decrypt incoming SSL traffic.

Generate Self-Signed Certificate

For testing, we can generate a self-signed certificate using OpenSSL:

```
openssl req -x509 -newkey rsa:4096 -keyout octavia.key -out
octavia.crt -days 365 -nodes
```

It generates a private key (**`octavia.key`**) and a self-signed certificate (**`octavia.crt`**) that is valid for 365 days.

During the generation process, we will be prompted to enter information such as the country, state, and common name (CN). The CN should match the domain name that clients will use to access the load balancer.

Create Certificate Bundle

The Octavia requires the private key and certificate to be combined into a single file, called a PEM (Privacy Enhanced Mail) file:

```
cat octavia.crt octavia.key > octavia.pem
```

It creates a PEM file (**octavia.pem**) containing both the certificate and the private key.

Configuring SSL Termination on Listener

With the certificate prepared, the next step is to configure SSL termination on an existing listener in Octavia.

The following creates a listener that uses SSL termination:

```
openstack loadbalancer listener create --name gitforgits-https-listener --protocol HTTPS --protocol-port 443 --loadbalancer gitforgits-lb --default-tls-container-ref <container_ref>
```

In the above, we need to replace **<container_ref>** with the actual reference to the container where the SSL certificate is stored. If we are using Barbican, we would first upload the PEM file to Barbican and use its container reference here as shown below:

```
openstack secret store --name octavia-cert --payload-content-type='application/octet-stream' --payload="$(cat octavia.pem)" --secret-type='certificate'
```

After this, we then retrieve the container reference:

```
openstack secret container create --name octavia-cert-container --secret octavia-cert
```

We can then use the output from the above script as the **container_ref** when creating the listener.

Next, we need to verify the configuration:

```
openstack loadbalancer listener show gitforgits-https-listener
```

Here, we just need to check that the listener is configured to use the HTTPS protocol, is listening on port 443, and is associated with the correct TLS container.

Testing SSL Termination

Once the SSL termination is configured, it is needed to test it to ensure that it's working as expected.

Access Load Balancer via HTTPS

We will make use of **curl** to test accessing the load balancer over HTTPS:

```
curl -k https://<vip_ip>
```

The response should indicate that the request has been routed through the load balancer and handled by one of the backend servers.

Verify SSL Termination

To confirm that SSL termination is working correctly, we will inspect the traffic on the backend servers. Since SSL termination is handled by the load balancer, the traffic between the load balancer and the backend servers should be unencrypted HTTP.

```
sudo tail -f /var/log/apache2/access.log
```

Here, the logs should show incoming HTTP requests from the load balancer, confirming that SSL was terminated at the load balancer and forwarded as HTTP to the backend.

Recipe 5: Integrating Octavia with Neutron Networking

Neutron provides connectivity as a service for other OpenStack services. Octavia relies heavily on Neutron to manage the network connectivity for load balancers, including the creation and management of VIPs, subnet attachments, and the routing of traffic to backend servers.

In this recipe, we will focus on integrating Octavia with the existing Neutron setup. This includes configuring the network resources that Octavia requires and ensuring that load balancers are correctly connected to the Neutron-managed networks.

Existing Neutron Networks

Before integrating Octavia with Neutron, it's important to understand the existing network setup within Neutron. This will help in planning how the load balancers will interact with the networks and subnets already in use.

List Existing Networks and Subnets

Here, we will list the existing networks and subnets in Neutron:

```
openstack network list
```

```
openstack subnet list
```

It provides a list of all networks and subnets currently configured in Neutron. Identify the network that will be used for the load balancer's VIP and the networks to which the backend servers are connected.

Review Network Configuration

And, we will now examine the details of the selected network and subnet to ensure they meet the requirements for load balancer integration:

```
openstack network show <network_id>
openstack subnet show <subnet_id>
```

Configuring Management Network

The Octavia requires a dedicated management network to communicate with the amphorae (the virtual machines that perform the load balancing). This network is used for health monitoring, control plane traffic, and other internal communications.

Create Management Network

If a management network does not already exist, we will create then one:

```
openstack network create octavia-mgmt-net
```

It creates a new network named **octavia-mgmt-net** for managing the Octavia amphorae.

Create Subnet for Management Network

Next, we will then create a subnet within the management network:

```
openstack subnet create --network octavia-mgmt-net --subnet-range 192.168.100.0/24 --gateway 192.168.100.1 octavia-mgmt-subnet
```

It creates a subnet named **octavia-mgmt-subnet** within the **octavia-mgmt-net** network, with the specified IP range.

Verify Management Network Configuration

Here, we will now confirm if the management network and subnet are correctly configured:

```
openstack network show octavia-mgmt-net
```

```
openstack subnet show octavia-mgmt-subnet
```

After this, we will ensure that the network and subnet are active and that the subnet configuration is correct.

Configuring Security Groups

The security groups in Neutron control the traffic allowed to and from instances, including the amphorae managed by Octavia.

So here, we will create a dedicated security group for the Octavia management network:

```
openstack security group create octavia-mgmt-secgroup --
description "Security group for Octavia management network"
```

After this, we then add the necessary rules to allow traffic between the Octavia services and the amphorae:

```
openstack security group rule create --protocol tcp --dst-port
22:22 --remote-ip 192.168.100.0/24 octavia-mgmt-secgroup

openstack security group rule create --protocol icmp octavia-
mgmt-secgroup

openstack security group rule create --protocol tcp --dst-port
9443:9443 --remote-ip 192.168.100.0/24 octavia-mgmt-secgroup
```

Here, the first rule allows SSH traffic on port 22. The second rule allows ICMP traffic (for ping). And, the third rule allows HTTPS traffic on port 9443, which is used for Octavia's API and management traffic.

Configuring Neutron for Octavia Integration

With the management network and security groups in place, the next step is to configure Neutron to work seamlessly with Octavia.

So here, we will update the Neutron configuration file (**/etc/neutron/neutron.conf**) to include settings specific to Octavia:

```
sudo nano /etc/neutron/neutron.conf
```

In the **[service_providers]** section, we then confirm if the Octavia is listed as the provider for LBaaS:

```
[service_providers]
```

```
service_provider=LOADBALANCER:Octavia:octavia_driver:default
```

After this, we then restart the Neutron services to apply the configuration changes:

```
sudo systemctl restart neutron-server
```

Deploying Load Balancer with Neutron Integration

With Octavia and Neutron fully integrated, we can now proceed to deploy a load balancer and verify that it works within the Neutron-managed networks.

The following one creates a new load balancer within a Neutron network:

```
openstack loadbalancer create --name gitforgits-lb --vip-subnet-id <subnet_id>
```

Next, we then create a listener for the load balancer:

```
openstack loadbalancer listener create --name gitforgits-http-listener --protocol HTTP --protocol-port 80 --loadbalancer gitforgits-lb
```

Next, we then create a pool and add backend servers to the load balancer:

```
openstack loadbalancer pool create --name gitforgits-pool --lb-algorithm ROUND_ROBIN --listener gitforgits-http-listener --protocol HTTP

openstack loadbalancer member create --subnet-id <subnet_id> --address <server_ip> --protocol-port 80 gitforgits-pool
```

It sets up a pool with a round-robin load balancing algorithm and adds members (backend servers) to it. And then verify that the load balancer is functioning correctly within the Neutron-managed network.

With this integration, the load balancers can efficiently distribute traffic across backend servers while fully utilizing the networking capabilities provided by Neutron.

Summary

To sum it up, we learned to use Octavia to balance the workload and make applications more reliable and perform better. We started by installing and setting up Octavia as the LBaaS solution. Next, we looked at how to create and manage load balancer pools, which help distribute traffic to backend servers using algorithms like round-robin.

We also learned to set up load balancer listeners and VIPs for directing traffic to the right backend servers. We put SSL termination in place to take on encryption and decryption tasks, moving them from backend servers to the load balancer. Lastly, we made sure that Octavia worked perfectly with the current network setup by integrating it with Neutron. As part of the integration, we also configured a dedicated management network, set up security groups, and verified that load balancers could function properly within the networks managed by Neutron.

Chapter 8: Managing Infrastructure using Terraform + IaC

Introduction

In this chapter, we will move our OpenStack infrastructure workflow into Terraform and will learn to replace manual resource creation with IaC for day-to-day cloud operations. We will begin by preparing Terraform for OpenStack through the provider configuration, authentication model, region selection, and the core CLI lifecycle so we can build with confidence from the first configuration onward. Once that foundation is in place, we will start defining cloud resources as code instead of building them one command at a time. This shift will help us make our infrastructure easier to review, repeat, modify, and clean up.

As we continue through the chapter, we will create networks, subnets, routers, router interfaces, and floating IPs with Terraform, and then we will extend that same workflow into compute and storage. We will provision key pairs, security groups, security group rules, and Nova instances, and we will connect them directly to the Terraform-managed network layer. After that, we will define Cinder volumes and attachment workflows so our compute resources gain persistent storage that is also managed through Terraform state. We will then organize the configuration into reusable parts through variables, outputs, locals, and logical units for network, compute, and storage. By the end of the chapter, we will be well versed to create infrastructure with Terraform, and also to update it, verify it, troubleshoot failures, handle drift, and clean it up safely.

Recipe 1: Setting up Terraform for OpenStack

In this chapter, we are no longer building around Heat stacks or Ceilometer-driven orchestration logic. That older model depends on additional OpenStack control-plane services and template-specific workflows. However, the Terraform lets us manage OpenStack resources from outside the control plane through a provider-based Infrastructure as Code workflow. The OpenStack provider on the Terraform Registry is built to interact with OpenStack resources directly, and the Terraform CLI workflow centers on a small, repeatable sequence of commands such as init, validate, plan, and apply. That shift is important for us because it simplifies how we build infrastructure for GitforGits.

We no longer need to prepare and maintain a separate orchestration service path just to define networks, instances, and volumes. Instead, we describe infrastructure in Terraform files, authenticate against OpenStack, and let Terraform calculate and execute the resource changes. That makes Terraform the right fit for the rest of this chapter, because our focus now moves from control-plane orchestration to declarative infrastructure management with a cleaner workflow and a wider ecosystem around reusable configuration patterns.

Terraform Working Directory

The Terraform expects configuration files in the current working directory, and terraform init prepares that directory by installing the required provider plugins and initializing Terraform's working data. HashiCorp's CLI reference states that terraform init is the first command we should run after writing or cloning configuration, and that it is safe to run multiple times as the configuration evolves. That behavior works well for us because it gives us a stable loop while we expand the chapter from provider setup into networks, compute, and storage.

To begin with, we will create a directory for the OpenStack Terraform work, enter it, and create a file named main.tf. We will start small and keep the configuration readable. Our first goal is not to provision a large environment.Rather, it is to prove that Terraform can talk to our OpenStack cloud cleanly and that we understand the CLI lifecycle well enough to move forward with confidence.

```
mkdir terraform-openstack
cd terraform-openstack
touch main.tf
Now place the following minimal configuration in main.tf:
terraform {
  required_providers {
    openstack = {
      source  = "terraform-provider-openstack/openstack"
    }
  }
}

provider "openstack" {
  region = "RegionOne"
}
```

This file tells Terraform that our working directory depends on the OpenStack provider and that our target region is RegionOne, which is the same region identifier we have already been using across the OpenStack control plane.

Authenticating with 'clouds.yaml'

The cleanest authentication path for OpenStack provider work is to use a clouds.yaml file together with the OS_CLOUD environment variable. This is a much more maintainable path for us because our later recipes will reuse the same authentication model without rewriting provider secrets repeatedly. So here, we will create **~/.config/openstack/clouds.yaml** and place the OpenStack cloud definition inside it. The values must match our controller endpoint, project, domain, username, password, and region. After saving the file, we then export **OS_CLOUD** so Terraform knows which named cloud entry to use when the provider initializes.

```
clouds:
  gitforgits:
    auth:
      auth_url: http://controller:5000/v3
      username: admin
      password: StrongPassword
      project_name: admin
      user_domain_name: Default
      project_domain_name: Default
    region_name: RegionOne
    interface: public
    identity_api_version: 3
export OS_CLOUD=gitforgits
```

At this point, our Terraform provider block remains short, readable, and region-aware while authentication stays outside the Terraform code itself.

Authenticating with Explicit Provider Arguments

The OpenStack provider supports explicit arguments such as auth_url, user_name, password, tenant_name, and domain settings, so this path remains valid when a clouds.yaml file is not available. We should still treat this as the less elegant path because credentials become part of the Terraform configuration itself, but it is useful to know it because many teams begin this way during initial testing. If we use explicit arguments, the region still belongs in the provider block, and Terraform will use those values directly when it initializes the provider.

So, here in the below, we will replace our earlier provider block with the following only if we intentionally want inline authentication. We should not keep both authentication styles active at once in the same configuration because clarity matters more than flexibility during early Terraform work.

```
provider "openstack" {
  auth_url    = "http://controller:5000/v3"
```

```
  user_name    = "admin"
  password     = "StrongPassword"
  tenant_name = "admin"
  domain_name = "Default"
  region       = "RegionOne"
}
```

This option is useful for fast lab validation, but the **clouds.yaml** pattern remains the better day-to-day path because it keeps credentials outside the Terraform configuration and aligns neatly with the OpenStack client behavior we already use elsewhere.

Running 'init', 'validate', 'plan', and 'apply'

After this, we are ready for the Terraform CLI lifecycle that will carry the rest of the chapter. The HashiCorp defines the **terraform init** as the command that initializes the working directory and installs providers, **terraform validate** as the command that checks whether the configuration files are syntactically and structurally valid, **terraform plan** as the command that shows the changes required to reach the declared state, and **terraform apply** as the command that executes the approved plan. Such a sequence is the heartbeat of Terraform work, and we should get comfortable with it now because we will reuse it again and again as we move into networks, instances, and volumes.

Now, since our current configuration contains only the provider block and no actual resources yet, the apply step should complete without creating anything.

```
terraform init
terraform validate
terraform plan -out tfplan
terraform apply tfplan
```

After running, here,if we get a clean run here, then it tells us that the Terraform can parse our configuration, initialize the OpenStack provider, authenticate using the method we selected, and move through the full execution lifecycle without errors. That means our working directory is ready for the real infrastructure resources that follow in the next recipes.

Recipe 2: Creating Networks, Subnets, Routers, and Floating IPs using Terraform

We already have a Terraform-managed internal network, subnet, router, router interface, and floating IP allocation path. What we need now is a secure and repeatable way to place Nova instances onto that network.

So here, we will do that by defining a key pair for SSH access, creating a dedicated Neutron security group with rules for SSH and ICMP, provisioning one or more Nova instances, and then attaching those instances to the Terraform-managed network using the network block inside the instance resource.

Key Pair and Security group

To start with, we will create a new file named compute.tf inside the same Terraform working directory. Our first job is to define access and protection before we create any server. The provider documentation for **openstack_compute_keypair_v2** states that it can either import a pre-generated public key or generate a key pair, but it also warns that generated private keys are stored unencrypted in Terraform state. For that reason, we will import an existing public key from our local SSH directory instead of asking Terraform to generate a private key for us. And then, we will define a Neutron security group and two rules, one for SSH on port 22 and one for ICMP so we can validate connectivity after the instance boots.

Following is the script that you should add to **compute.tf**:

```
resource "openstack_compute_keypair_v2" "gitforgits_key" {
  name       = "gitforgits-key"
  public_key = file("~/.ssh/id_rsa.pub")
}

resource "openstack_networking_secgroup_v2" "ssh_access" {
  name                 = "tf-ssh-secgroup"
  description          = "Security group for SSH and ping
access"
  delete_default_rules = true
}

resource "openstack_networking_secgroup_rule_v2" "egress_ipv4"
{
  direction         = "egress"
  ethertype         = "IPv4"
```

```
  security_group_id =
openstack_networking_secgroup_v2.ssh_access.id
}

resource "openstack_networking_secgroup_rule_v2" "egress_ipv6"
{
  direction         = "egress"
  ethertype         = "IPv6"
  security_group_id =
openstack_networking_secgroup_v2.ssh_access.id
}

resource "openstack_networking_secgroup_rule_v2" "ssh_ingress"
{
  direction         = "ingress"
  ethertype         = "IPv4"
  protocol          = "tcp"
  port_range_min    = 22
  port_range_max    = 22
  remote_ip_prefix  = "0.0.0.0/0"
  security_group_id =
openstack_networking_secgroup_v2.ssh_access.id
}

resource "openstack_networking_secgroup_rule_v2"
"icmp_ingress" {
  direction         = "ingress"
  ethertype         = "IPv4"
  protocol          = "icmp"
  remote_ip_prefix  = "0.0.0.0/0"
```

```
  security_group_id =
openstack_networking_secgroup_v2.ssh_access.id
}
```

Provisioning Nova Instances on Terraform-managed Network

We will now create the compute instances. The OpenStack provider documentation for **openstack_compute_instance_v2** shows that an instance can reference an existing image and flavor, can use a previously created key pair, can associate one or more security groups by name, and can attach to a network through a network block. This is exactly what we need, because the network from our previous recipe already exists in Terraform state as **openstack_networking_network_v2.internal**.

So, to keep the workflow practical, we will define a small data source for the image we already uploaded earlier, and we will use the flavor name that we created during the Nova setup work. We will also create two instances instead of one so our environment is ready for later connectivity checks and storage work.

So, we just need to append the following to **compute.tf**:

```
data "openstack_images_image_v2" "cirros" {
  name        = "CirrOS"
  most_recent = true
}

resource "openstack_compute_instance_v2" "app_server_1" {
  name            = "tf-app-server-1"
  image_id        = data.openstack_images_image_v2.cirros.id
  flavor_name     = "m1.small"
  key_pair        =
openstack_compute_keypair_v2.gitforgits_key.name
  security_groups =
[openstack_networking_secgroup_v2.ssh_access.name]

  network {
    uuid = openstack_networking_network_v2.internal.id
```

```
  }
}

resource "openstack_compute_instance_v2" "app_server_2" {
  name            = "tf-app-server-2"
  image_id        = data.openstack_images_image_v2.cirros.id
  flavor_name     = "m1.small"
  key_pair        =
openstack_compute_keypair_v2.gitforgits_key.name
  security_groups =
[openstack_networking_secgroup_v2.ssh_access.name]

  network {
    uuid = openstack_networking_network_v2.internal.id
  }
}
```

Associating Floating IP to Terraform-managed Instance

From oner of the previous chapter, the network recipe already allocated a floating IP resource for us, so we will now connect that address to one of the instances we just created. So now, we will associate the existing floating IP from our previous recipe with the first application server. That gives us one externally reachable instance while still keeping the second instance internal to the tenant network.

```
data "openstack_networking_port_v2" "app_server_1_port" {
  device_id  = openstack_compute_instance_v2.app_server_1.id
  network_id = openstack_networking_network_v2.internal.id
}

resource "openstack_networking_floatingip_associate_v2"
"app_server_1_fip" {
```

```
  floating_ip =
openstack_networking_floatingip_v2.public_ip.address
  port_id     =
data.openstack_networking_port_v2.app_server_1_port.id
}


output "app_server_1_floating_ip" {
  value = openstack_networking_floatingip_v2.public_ip.address
}
```

Applying Compute Configuration

After this, we are ready to apply the full compute layer. Our Terraform directory already contains the provider setup and the network resources, so this recipe only adds the compute-specific parts.

So in this step, we will run **terraform validate** first so we catch missing references or syntax mistakes. Then, we continue with **terraform plan** so we can inspect the creation of the key pair, security group, rules, instances, port lookup, and floating IP association. And then, we finish with **terraform apply**, then use both Terraform output and the OpenStack CLI to verify what was created.

```
terraform validate
terraform plan -out tfplan
terraform apply tfplan
terraform output app_server_1_floating_ip

openstack keypair list
openstack security group list
openstack security group rule list tf-ssh-secgroup
openstack server list
openstack server show tf-app-server-1 -f value -c addresses
openstack server show tf-app-server-2 -f value -c addresses
openstack floating ip list
```

From the above, our main validation point is that, the key pair should exist in Nova, the security group should exist in Neutron with the expected rules, both instances should appear in Nova, both should attach to the Terraform-managed network, and the first instance should hold the floating IP allocated earlier. Once those checks pass, we know our Terraform workflow now covers both network and compute resources in a connected and reusable way

With this recipe completed, we are having a Terraform-managed compute foundation that sits directly on top of our Terraform-managed Neutron layer.

Recipe 3: Managing Cinder Volumes and Attachments

A Nova instance gives us compute capacity, but a Cinder volume gives us persistent block storage that can be attached, detached, and managed independently of the instance lifecycle. That distinction matters for GitforGits because application data should not disappear just because a server is rebuilt. In Terraform terms, this becomes even more valuable because the volume and its attachment are not one-off manual actions. They become part of the same state-managed workflow as the rest of our infrastructure.

So here, in this recipe, we will declare the volume resource, declare the attachment workflow, and Terraform keeps track of both so future plans can show whether anything is about to change.

Defining Cinder Volume in Terraform

We will continue in the same Terraform working directory that already contains our provider, networking, and compute resources. For this, we will again create a new file named **storage.tf**, and then we will define a Cinder volume resource that will belong to the same region and provider configuration we already established earlier.

So, the first step is to add the following script to **storage.tf**. It will declare a persistent volume for our first application instance.

```
resource "openstack_blockstorage_volume_v3" "app_data_volume"
{
  name = "tf-app-data-volume"
  size = 5
}


output "app_data_volume_id" {
  value = openstack_blockstorage_volume_v3.app_data_volume.id
```

```
}
```

This configuration will give us a dedicated 5 GB Cinder volume that Terraform will track in state. Because the volume exists as its own resource, we are not binding the data lifecycle tightly to the instance lifecycle.

Attaching Volume to Existing Instance

Next, we will connect the new volume to the Nova instance that we created in the previous recipe. The provider supports a volume attachment workflow through a compute-side attachment resource, and this allows us to attach the block storage volume directly to the instance resource we already manage in Terraform. Since **`tf-app-server-1`** already exists in our configuration as **`openstack_compute_instance_v2.app_server_1`**, we can reference that resource directly instead of typing IDs manually. That keeps the configuration clean and lets Terraform understand the dependency chain automatically.

The following script gets the volume attached to our first server:

```
resource "openstack_compute_volume_attach_v2"
"app_data_attach" {
  instance_id = openstack_compute_instance_v2.app_server_1.id
  volume_id   =
openstack_blockstorage_volume_v3.app_data_volume.id
}


output "app_server_1_volume_attachment" {
  value =
openstack_compute_volume_attach_v2.app_data_attach.id
}
```

This attachment turns our volume from an abstract storage object into a usable disk for the instance. The Terraform now understands that the server depends on the network path from earlier recipes and that the volume attachment depends on both the server and the Cinder volume. This dependency chain is exactly what makes the Terraform model so practical. We are not memorizing a sequence of manual storage commands. We are simply defining the desired state and allowing Terraform to manage the order and state of the underlying OpenStack actions.

Applying Storage Workflow

Since the provider and earlier resources are already in place, we only need to validate, plan, and apply the new storage additions. So here, we will run **terraform validate** first to catch syntax or reference issues. And then, we will run **terraform plan** to confirm that Terraform intends to create one block storage volume and one attachment. After that, we will apply the plan and display the volume output. Once the apply succeeds, we then validate the result from OpenStack side because our storage workflow should remain understandable in both Terraform and the native OpenStack view.

```
terraform validate
terraform plan -out tfplan
terraform apply tfplan
terraform output app_data_volume_id

openstack volume list
openstack volume show tf-app-data-volume
openstack server show tf-app-server-1 -f value -c
volumes_attached
```

All these above checks tell us whether the Terraform state and the OpenStack state agree. If they do, we have successfully moved from compute into managed persistent storage. That means our first application server now has a dedicated block device whose lifecycle is tracked in Terraform rather than being left to ad hoc attachment steps that are difficult to reproduce later.

Verifying Volume inside Instance

The final part of the workflow is to verify the attached block device from inside the guest. Since our earlier compute recipe already associated a floating IP with **tf-app-server-1**, we can use that same access path now. SSH into the instance with the key pair we created earlier, then inspect the block devices with **lsblk**. We expect to see a new disk in addition to the root disk.

We will run the following after retrieving the floating IP output from the previous recipe:

```
ssh -i ~/.ssh/id_rsa ubuntu@<app_server_1_floating_ip>
lsblk
```

With this step complete, we then have a persistent storage workflow that fits naturally into our Terraform-managed OpenStack environment. The volume is declared in code, the attachment is declared in code, Terraform state tracks both, OpenStack reflects both, and the guest operating system can see the resulting block device.

Recipe 4: Structuring Terraform for Reusable OpenStack Infrastructure

In general, the Terraform is designed around reusable building blocks, and its language gives us the tools to shape those building blocks cleanly through input variables, local values, output values, and child modules. The official Terraform documentation explains that variables define a module's input interface, outputs expose useful data, and locals help us reuse expressions inside a module without repeating them over and over. The Terraform's module model allows us to compose those units into a larger infrastructure layout while keeping each unit focused on one job. That is exactly the direction we should always look for GitforGits or for your any project, because the OpenStack environment already has natural boundaries such as network, compute, and storage.

Designing Reusable File Layout

We will begin by reshaping our Terraform directory into a layout that is easier to scale, where we assemble reusable units. A practical pattern is to keep a small root module with main.tf, variables.tf, outputs.tf, and terraform.tfvars, then create a modules directory with separate subdirectories such as network, compute, and storage.

Following is the best layout of our working directory:

```
terraform-openstack/
├── main.tf
├── variables.tf
├── outputs.tf
├── terraform.tfvars
└── modules/
    ├── network/
    │   ├── main.tf
    │   ├── variables.tf
    │   └── outputs.tf
    ├── compute/
    │   ├── main.tf
    │   ├── variables.tf
    │   └── outputs.tf
    └── storage/
        ├── main.tf
        ├── variables.tf
        └── outputs.tf
```

In the above layout, the network module owns the internal network, subnet, router, and floating

IP pool logic. The compute module owns the key pair, security groups, security group rules, instances, and floating IP association. And, the storage module owns the Cinder volumes and volume attachments. This separation keeps each concern focused and prevents the root configuration from turning into one long file that is difficult to maintain.

Using Variables and Locals to Remove Repetition

Variables are for values that we expect to change between environments or between runs, such as region name, internal subnet CIDR, flavor name, image name, key pair path, and volume size. The Terraform's variable documentation describes variables as the input interface for a module, which is exactly how we should think about them here.

The locals serve a different purpose. They are internal helpers inside a module, and Terraform's locals documentation recommends using them when we want to reuse an expression or give a repeated expression a meaningful name.

So here, we will create the root **`variables.tf`** with values we want to control centrally:

```
variable "region" {
  type        = string
  default     = "RegionOne"
  description = "OpenStack region for GitforGits resources"
}

variable "external_network_name" {
  type        = string
  default     = "ovn-ext-net"
  description = "Existing external provider network"
}

variable "internal_cidr" {
  type        = string
  default     = "192.168.50.0/24"
  description = "Internal subnet for GitforGits"
}
```

```
variable "image_name" {
  type        = string
  default     = "CirrOS"
  description = "Image name for compute instances"
}

variable "flavor_name" {
  type        = string
  default     = "m1.small"
  description = "Flavor name for compute instances"
}
```

After this, we then create a root **locals.tf** so repeated names stay consistent:

```
locals {
  environment_prefix = "gitforgits"
  network_name       = "${local.environment_prefix}-internal-
net"
  subnet_name        = "${local.environment_prefix}-internal-
subnet"
  router_name        = "${local.environment_prefix}-router"
  secgroup_name      = "${local.environment_prefix}-ssh-
secgroup"
  volume_name        = "${local.environment_prefix}-app-data-
volume"
}
```

Splitting Network, Compute, and Storage into Logical Units

We will now proceed to wire the modules together from the root configuration. The network module should accept values such as region, external network name, internal network name, subnet name, and internal CIDR. Its outputs should expose values such as internal network ID, subnet ID, router ID, and floating IP address. The compute module should accept image name, flavor name, internal network ID, security group name, and optionally a floating IP if we want the first instance to be reachable from outside. The storage module should accept the instance ID that needs a volume, along with volume name and size. The Terraform's module documentation explains that child modules communicate with the parent through inputs and outputs, and that is exactly how our GitforGits layout should behave.

Following is how our root **main.tf** should look like:

```
module "network" {
  source                = "./modules/network"
  region                = var.region
  external_network_name = var.external_network_name
  network_name          = local.network_name
  subnet_name           = local.subnet_name
  router_name           = local.router_name
  internal_cidr         = var.internal_cidr
}

module "compute" {
  source          = "./modules/compute"
  region          = var.region
  image_name      = var.image_name
  flavor_name     = var.flavor_name
  network_id      = module.network.network_id
  security_group  = local.secgroup_name
  floating_ip     = module.network.floating_ip_address
}

module "storage" {
  source      = "./modules/storage"
  region      = var.region
  instance_id = module.compute.app_server_1_id
  volume_name = local.volume_name
```

```
  volume_size = 5
}
```

In the above, the network produces IDs that compute needs, and compute produces instance IDs that storage needs. Such dependency chain stays visible and intentional instead of being scattered across unrelated files.

Exposing Outputs and Validating Layout

The outputs complete the reusable workflow because they expose the values that other modules or operators need after an apply. So here, we should expose values such as network ID, subnet ID, router ID, floating IP address, instance IDs, and volume ID. These values are going to be the glue that keeps our modules useful and our future recipes manageable. Once we add outputs in each module and in the root module, the Terraform workflow stays exactly the same as before.

So here, we will run the same lifecycle from the root directory:

```
terraform validate
terraform plan -out tfplan
terraform apply tfplan
terraform output
```

With this, we have variables for environment-specific values, locals for repeated expressions, outputs for sharing useful attributes, a clear file layout, and logical modules that divide the OpenStack environment into network, compute, and storage units. That gives us a reusable Terraform foundation rather than a growing collection of unrelated resource blocks.

Recipe 5: Troubleshooting Terraform-managed OpenStack Infrastructure

When we worked with orchestration-oriented workflows in the past, we often had to think in terms of stack failures, rollback states, partial resource creation, and delete failures. In Terraform, the operating model is different, but the operational problems still exist in their own form. Instead of a Heat stack entering a failed or rollback state, the Terraform gives us configuration validation errors, plan-time failures, apply-time failures, drift between state and the real cloud, and destroy operations that stop because a dependency is still in the way.

This recipe is going to teach us managing apply-time failures, validation issues, drift, and delete failures and not them turn into a chaotic mess.

Catching Validation and Plan-time Errors

Our first line of defense is to stop bad configuration before it touches OpenStack at all. And to do this, we should begin with **terraform validate**, then run **terraform plan**, and then inspect the resulting plan carefully. We can also use **terraform show** to inspect the saved plan in human-readable form before apply.

```
terraform validate
terraform plan -out tfplan
terraform show tfplan
terraform apply tfplan
```

If **terraform validate** fails, then we fix the configuration before doing anything else. If **terraform plan** shows an unexpected destroy or replacement, then we can try to review the variables, module inputs, and resource references before proceeding. Here, our best protection is to avoid the accidental infrastructure damage.

Handling Apply-Time Failures, Partial Creation, and Drift

An apply can still fail even after a good plan, because OpenStack may reject an operation due to quota limits, missing dependencies, port conflicts, attachment ordering, or a mismatch between Terraform state and real infrastructure. So here, when a failure happens, we need to be little methodical. We will first inspect the OpenStack side using OpenStack CLI to see whether any part of the resource was actually created. Then, we will inspect Terraform state to see whether that resource is recorded. And then, we will compare the two before making changes. If the real cloud changed outside Terraform, then my best practice is **refresh-only** mode through **terraform plan -refresh-only** or **terraform apply -refresh-only** rather than deprecated standalone **terraform refresh** command. It gives us a clean path for drift reconciliation when a resource exists but its current attributes no longer match the state Terraform has stored.

```
terraform state list
terraform state show
openstack_compute_instance_v2.app_server_1
terraform plan -refresh-only
terraform apply -refresh-only
openstack server list
openstack volume list
```

```
openstack network list
```

If the OpenStack object exists but Terraform does not track it, then we can bring it under management instead of recreating blindly.

Overcoming State Mismatches and Failed Delete Operations

The delete failures are the Terraform equivalent of old orchestration cleanup failures. They usually happen because a resource still has a dependency attached to it. A router may still own an interface, a floating IP may still be associated with a port, or a volume may still be attached to an instance.

So, in such cases, we can inspect the resource and the live OpenStack object, and then we can decide, should we detach something in OpenStack or remove something from state itself.

```
terraform state show
openstack_networking_router_interface_v2.internal

openstack router show tf-internal-router

openstack floating ip list

openstack volume show tf-app-data-volume

terraform plan -refresh-only

terraform apply -refresh-only

terraform destroy
```

In the above, if a volume refuses to delete because it is still attached, we can detach it first through the OpenStack side or by correcting the Terraform attachment resource. If a router refuses to delete because its interface still exists, then we can remove the router interface dependency in configuration.

At this point, we have a full Terraform operating model for GitforGits rather than only a creation model. We know how to validate configuration before execution, how to inspect a saved plan before applying it, how to trace apply-time failures through Terraform state and OpenStack CLI output, how to reconcile drift with refresh-only mode, how to inspect managed resources with terraform state list and terraform state show, how to adopt existing resources through import workflows, and how to recover from cleanup failures by resolving dependency chains before retrying destroy.

Summary

This chapter shifted our infrastructure workflow from control-plane orchestration to declarative Infrastructure as Code with Terraform for OpenStack. We began by preparing Terraform to work with our cloud through the provider block, region selection, and authentication using clouds.yaml or explicit provider arguments. From there, we learned the Terraform CLI lifecycle through init, validate, plan, and apply, and we saw how that workflow gave us a predictable way to review and execute infrastructure changes. We then created OpenStack networking resources as code, including internal networks, subnets, routers, router interfaces, and floating IPs, while keeping continuity with the Neutron topology we had already built earlier through the command line.

After building the network layer, we moved into compute and storage and then into reusable Terraform design. We provisioned key pairs, security groups, security group rules, and Nova instances, and we attached those instances to the Terraform-managed network instead of creating them manually. We then added persistent block storage by declaring a Cinder volume and attaching it to an instance through Terraform so the storage lifecycle became state-managed and repeatable. Finally, we organized the environment into reusable network, compute, and storage units through variables, outputs, locals, and a reusable file layout, and we closed the chapter by learning how updates, validation problems, drift, partial failures, state inspection, and cleanup operations could be handled in a controlled and recoverable way.

Chapter 9: Telemetry and Monitoring using Gnocchi + Prometheus

Introduction

In this chapter, we will build a practical telemetry and monitoring path using Gnocchi and Prometheus. We begin by learning the role of Gnocchi in our cloud, how it stores the measurements as time-series data, and why it serves as the metrics layer for our environment. After that, we will install and configure Gnocchi so that it works with our cloud services and gives us a reliable place to keep operational measurements. Once the setup is complete, we will move from service preparation into actual metric work so that we can create, store, retrieve, and validate sample measurements instead of stopping at installation alone.

As we continue through the chapter, we will use Gnocchi to work with metrics, measures, archive policies, and aggregations so that our service health visibility becomes practical and testable. After that, we will bring in Prometheus and the OpenStack Exporter so that our cloud metrics can be scraped, queried, and watched from a broader monitoring layer. We will configure scrape jobs, work with key OpenStack metrics, and add a small alerting rule that will help us identify monitoring problems quickly. We will also shape a compact dashboard-style view so that the GitforGits gains a usable monitoring surface rather than just a collection of raw measurements. By the end of the chapter, we will have a complete and usable workflow for telemetry, metric validation, cloud monitoring, and alert-driven visibility.

Recipe 1: Installing and Configuring Gnocchi

Gnocchi is the metrics storage layer we will use for this chapter. Its job is to store and index time series data at scale, which makes it a strong fit for cloud infrastructure where measurements arrive continuously and where resources such as instances, networks, and volumes may change over time. Gnocchi works with a simple but powerful model. A metric receives measures, which are timestamp and value pairs, and those measures are then aggregated according to an archive policy. The archive policy defines how frequently aggregates are computed and how long they are retained. Gnocchi documentation describes it as a time series database focused on storage and indexing of metrics and resources, and it also describes archive policies as the mechanism that controls granularity, retention, and aggregations such as average, minimum, and maximum. This means Gnocchi is not just a bucket for raw numbers. It is the place where our cloud metrics become queryable, retained, and meaningful over time.

How Gnocchi Stores Metrics?

We should understand the storage model before we install anything, because that will make the configuration choices feel natural rather than arbitrary. Gnocchi separates its concerns into a resource indexer, a storage backend, and metric processing workers. The official documentation describes support for PostgreSQL for the indexer, support for different storage drivers such as file or Ceph, and support for Keystone for authentication. It also documents that default archive policies such as low, medium, high, and bool are created during the upgrade step, and that these policies control how much data is kept and at what granularity.

For GitforGits, we will keep the setup practical and compact by using PostgreSQL as the indexer and file-based metric storage so the chapter remains easy to follow on a small OpenStack environment.

Installing Gnocchi Packages

The official OpenStack telemetry installation for Ubuntu shows that Gnocchi packages can be installed through the system package manager using **gnocchi-api**, **gnocchi-metricd**, and **python3-gnocchiclient**. We will use that path because it keeps our environment aligned with the rest of our **controller-node** package workflow. We will also prepare PostgreSQL support for the indexer and Apache support for the API service endpoint on the controller.

So here, our target is a controller-hosted Gnocchi service that authenticates through Keystone and stores metrics locally on disk for this GitforGits deployment. Since this is our first-time Gnocchi installation in this book, this is the one place where we will introduce the package installation commands as shown below:

```
sudo apt update

sudo apt install -y gnocchi-api gnocchi-metricd python3-
gnocchiclient postgresql apache2 libapache2-mod-wsgi-py3
```

Creating Gnocchi Database and Keystone Identity

We now need to give Gnocchi its database and service identity so it can operate as a first-class OpenStack service. The Gnocchi installation documentation shows PostgreSQL as a supported indexer backend, and the same installation material includes Keystone support as an installation variant, which matches the identity flow we have already been using across Keystone, Nova, Neutron, and Cinder.

So now, we will create a PostgreSQL database and user for Gnocchi, then register the service user in Keystone and create the API service and endpoints. We will use the same password discipline that we have used throughout the book so the control-plane layout remains consistent.

```
sudo -u postgres psql

CREATE DATABASE gnocchi;

CREATE USER gnocchi WITH PASSWORD 'StrongPassword';

GRANT ALL PRIVILEGES ON DATABASE gnocchi TO gnocchi;

\q
```

```
. admin-openrc

openstack user create --domain default --password-prompt
gnocchi

openstack role add --project service --user gnocchi admin

openstack service create --name gnocchi --description "Metric
Service" metric

openstack endpoint create --region RegionOne metric public
http://controller:8041

openstack endpoint create --region RegionOne metric internal
http://controller:8041

openstack endpoint create --region RegionOne metric admin
http://controller:8041
```

Configuring Gnocchi for PostgreSQL, File Storage, and Keystone

Our main configuration work now happens in **/etc/gnocchi/gnocchi.conf**. So now, we will set the indexer to PostgreSQL, the storage backend to file, and the authentication mode to Keystone. We will also define a file storage path that Gnocchi can write to safely.

```
[indexer]
url = postgresql://gnocchi:StrongPassword@controller/gnocchi

[storage]
driver = file
file_basepath = /var/lib/gnocchi

[api]
auth_mode = keystone

[keystone_authtoken]
auth_url = http://controller:5000/v3
www_authenticate_uri = http://controller:5000/v3
```

```
memcached_servers = controller:11211
auth_type = password
project_domain_name = Default
user_domain_name = Default
project_name = service
username = gnocchi
password = StrongPassword
sudo mkdir -p /var/lib/gnocchi
sudo chown -R gnocchi:gnocchi /var/lib/gnocchi
```

Initializing and Verifying Service Metrics Store

After this, we are ready to initialize the database schema, create the default archive policies, and start the service processes. So here, we will enable the metric processing service and restart Apache so the API becomes reachable on the endpoint we registered in Keystone.

```
sudo gnocchi-upgrade
sudo systemctl enable gnocchi-metricd
sudo systemctl restart gnocchi-metricd
sudo systemctl restart apache2

. admin-openrc
gnocchi status
gnocchi archive-policy list
```

In the above, if the archive policies appear, then wecan say that the GitforGits metrics store is live and ready for the next recipe where we will query and validate actual metrics.

Recipe 2: Querying and Validating Metrics

We will now move to metric work. In general, the Gnocchi organizes data around metrics, measures, archive policies, and aggregations. A metric is the named thing we want to observe, such as CPU usage, request rate, queue depth, or service availability. The measures are the timestamped values we send into that metric. And the archive policies define the retention and granularity model, which means they decide how long data lives and at what resolution it is stored.

In my understanding, the default archive policies such as low, medium, high, and bool are created during the upgrade step, which gives us a ready baseline without creating a custom policy first.

Listing Archive Policies and Creating Metric

Next, we try to list archive policies so we know what retention choices are available. After that, we create a sample metric which will represent a small operational signal, and we will store it under the medium archive policy so we get practical retention without creating a custom rule yet.

```
. admin-openrc
gnocchi archive-policy list
gnocchi metric create --archive-policy-name medium --name
gitforgits.api.response_time
gnocchi metric list
gnocchi metric show gitforgits.api.response_time
```

In the above, once the metric is created, we need to keep its ID or name visible because we can use it again in the next steps when we want to add measures and query them back.

Adding and Reading Sample Measures

Now that we have a metric, our next step is to feed measures. So, a measure is just a timestamp paired with a numeric value, and this is where Gnocchi starts feeling useful. Here, we will insert a short sequence of sample response time values into **`gitforgits.api.response_time`** metric.

After the measures are added, we will immediately request them back with metric measures show so we can confirm that the data path is healthy. This small loop is very important because it proves that authentication works, metric creation worked, ingestion works, and retrieval works.

```
gnocchi measures add --metric gitforgits.api.response_time \
  --measure "2026-03-16T10:00:00+00:00" 120.0 \
  --measure "2026-03-16T10:01:00+00:00" 180.0 \
  --measure "2026-03-16T10:02:00+00:00" 140.0 \
  --measure "2026-03-16T10:03:00+00:00" 220.0 \
  --measure "2026-03-16T10:04:00+00:00" 160.0

gnocchi measures show --metric gitforgits.api.response_time
```

In the above script, we shall keep the metric name the same so the later aggregation step can be built on the exact data.

Working with Aggregations and Time Windows

The raw measures are useful, but cloud monitoring becomes much more meaningful when we query aggregates across a time window. This Gnocchi supports aggregation retrieval and cross-metric aggregation.

For our GitforGits sample metric, we will request aggregated values over the same period we just loaded. We will ask for the average and maximum at a one-minute granularity so we can see how the metric would look in a service-health check rather than in a per-measure ingest view.

```
gnocchi measures show \
  --metric gitforgits.api.response_time \
  --aggregation mean \
  --granularity 60 \
  --start 2026-03-16T10:00:00+00:00 \
  --stop 2026-03-16T10:05:00+00:00

gnocchi measures show \
  --metric gitforgits.api.response_time \
  --aggregation max \
  --granularity 60 \
  --start 2026-03-16T10:00:00+00:00 \
  --stop 2026-03-16T10:05:00+00:00
```

After the above commands, the Gnocchi becomes a real telemetry backend for us. It lets us move from a stream of numbers into a summarized operational signal.

Using Gnocchi for Service Health Visibility

A service health signal becomes easier to understand when we treat the metric as a living operational indicator rather than a one-time data sample. For example, the response time can tell us whether the API tier is staying under control or moving toward stress. The Gnocchi also exposes a service-side health view. Its release notes mention the **`/healthcheck`** endpoint for API service health, and the shell utility includes a status command that gives us a quick look at the service side from the CLI.

Here, it gives us two angles of validation:

- One angle checks whether Gnocchi itself is healthy. And,
- the other checks whether the project metric we care about is being stored and queried correctly.

The following validates the service side and the metric side in the same workflow.

```
gnocchi status

curl -s http://controller:8041/healthcheck

gnocchi metric show gitforgits.api.response_time

gnocchi measures show --metric gitforgits.api.response_time --
aggregation mean --granularity 60
```

The real value of this solution, is that, it turned Gnocchi into a usable metrics store. We can define a metric, feed it data, ask useful questions of it, and confirm that the metrics service itself is healthy. In the next recipe, we will make use of Prometheus to provide a broader monitoring path of our OpenStack infrastructure.

Recipe 3: Monitoring OpenStack with Prometheus and OpenStack Exporter

The Prometheus provides a pull-based monitoring layer for our OpenStack environment. And, the OpenStack Exporter acts as the bridge that exposes cloud metrics in a format Prometheus can scrape. The exporter project describes itself as a service that exposes metrics from a running OpenStack cloud for Prometheus consumption, and it states that credentials should use the os-client-config format through a **clouds.yaml** file. The Prometheus itself expects scrape targets to expose metrics on an HTTP endpoint, most commonly at **/metrics**, and it uses **scrape_configs** in **prometheus.yml** to define how those targets are collected.

So, in this recipe, we will prepare the exporter, expose its metrics endpoint, then point the Prometheus at that endpoint, and later we will use a small alerting rule and a compact dashboard view for real service visibility over the traditional raw metric collection.

Setting up OpenStack Exporter

To start with, we will create a dedicated working area for the exporter. The exporter's README if we could refer to, it states that it reads **clouds.yaml** through the **--os-client-config** flag and can bind its own HTTP service so Prometheus can scrape it. If this is true, then we do not need a special OpenStack authentication pattern for monitoring at all.

So here, we will reuse the standard cloud definition and then run the exporter on port 9180.

```
clouds:
  gitforgits:
    auth:
      auth_url: http://controller:5000/v3
      username: admin
      password: StrongPassword
      project_name: admin
      user_domain_name: Default
      project_domain_name: Default
    region_name: RegionOne
    interface: public
    identity_api_version: 3
sudo mkdir -p /etc/openstack
sudo vi /etc/openstack/clouds.yaml

./openstack-exporter \
  --os-client-config /etc/openstack/clouds.yaml \
  --web.listen-address=:9180
curl http://controller:9180/metrics | head
```

Once the exporter is running, and if we open the **/metrics** endpoint, we can confirm that the Prometheus-format metric lines are being exposed before we even touch the Prometheus server itself.

Configuring Prometheus Scraping

At this point, the Prometheus needs only a valid scrape job that points to the exporter. So here, we will therefore add one scrape job for Prometheus itself and one scrape job for the OpenStack Exporter.

```
global:
  scrape_interval: 15s
```

```
scrape_configs:
  - job_name: prometheus
    static_configs:
      - targets: ["localhost:9090"]

  - job_name: openstack_exporter
    static_configs:
      - targets: ["controller:9180"]
sudo systemctl restart prometheus
sudo systemctl status prometheus --no-pager
```

This gives us immediate visibility into both the monitoring server and the cloud exporter without introducing any advanced service discovery mechanism. In the above, after the restart, the Targets page shows the **openstack_exporter** job in the **UP** state. And this confirms that the exporter is reachable and the Prometheus scrape loop is active.

Working with OpenStack Metrics

After the target is **UP**, the Prometheus begins storing the exporter's time series and we can start asking useful operational questions. In practice, the first metrics we should care about are the cloud's view of instances, floating IPs, hypervisors, quotas, and service availability, because these metrics tell us whether our cloud is healthy enough to accept or support workloads.

So now, we open the Prometheus expression browser and look for broad metric name searches such as **openstack_** so we can discover the exact metric names present in our exporter build.

Following is the Prometheus expressions we may try:

```
{job="openstack_exporter"}

up{job="openstack_exporter"}

openstack_nova_vcpus_available
openstack_nova_memory_available_bytes
openstack_neutron_floating_ips
openstack_cinder_volumes
```

In the above, the goal is not to memorize every metric. The goal is just to identify a small operational set that tells us whether GitforGits **compute**, **networking**, and **capacity** remain healthy and available.

Creating Alerting Rule

The metrics become much more valuable once they can trigger attention when something goes wrong. So here, we will create a rule file named **openstack-alerts.yml**, and will add the following alert, and then reference that rule file from **prometheus.yml**.

```
groups:
  - name: openstack_alerts
    rules:
      - alert: OpenStackExporterDown
        expr: up{job="openstack_exporter"} == 0
        for: 1m
        labels:
          severity: warning
        annotations:
          summary: OpenStack Exporter is unreachable
          description: Prometheus has failed to scrape the
OpenStack exporter for more than one minute.
```

Next, we then need to add the following to the **prometheus.yml**:

```
rule_files:
  - /etc/prometheus/openstack-alerts.yml
```

After reloading Prometheus, we can visit the Alerts page in the web interface and can see that the rule is loaded. This is a very effective monitoring checkpoint, because the exporter's health becomes visible immediately and the alert will fire if Prometheus cannot scrape it for more than one minute. We can extend this later with quota or service-capacity alerts, but this first rule gives us the right operational pattern to build on.

Building Compact Dashboard View

Finally, we need a small dashboard which is going to be a very useful dashboard showing exporter availability, instance-related metrics, hypervisor capacity visibility, floating IP totals, and Cinder volume counts. The Prometheus itself already provides the expression browser and graphing view, so even without a separate dashboard system, we can think to assemble a working operational screen from these queries.

To do this, we simply have to start by graphing **`up{job="openstack_exporter"}`** and a few key OpenStack metric expressions in separate panels. It standalone can give a usable operational surface for the cloud. Overall, with Prometheus scraping active, the exporter serving OpenStack metrics, and one alert rule loaded, we can have a monitoring path that is simple to understand and practical to extend.

Summary

In this chapter, we worked through a practical monitoring path for our OpenStack environment by combining Gnocchi with Prometheus. We began by learning what Gnocchi did for us as a metrics storage layer and how it stored time-series measurements through metrics, measures, archive policies, and aggregations. After that foundation, we installed and configured Gnocchi for the GitforGits, connected it with Keystone authentication, and prepared it to store cloud measurements in a structured way. We then moved from setup into actual metric work by creating sample metrics, adding measures, retrieving them, and validating aggregated values so that service health visibility became something we could verify directly instead of assuming from service startup alone.

After building that metrics base, we extended our monitoring path with Prometheus and the OpenStack Exporter so that the cloud could expose operational signals in a scrape-friendly format. We configured the exporter with OpenStack credentials, connected Prometheus to it through a scrape job, and worked with key cloud-facing metrics related to service visibility and resource state. We also added a small alerting rule so that exporter unavailability could be detected quickly, and we shaped a compact dashboard view that focused on the metrics that mattered most for everyday cloud operations. By the end of the chapter, we had moved from raw telemetry concepts into a working monitoring workflow that covered storage, querying, scraping, alerting, and day-to-day visibility for our project.

Index

A

B

C

D

E

F

G

P

Q

R

S

T

V

W

Thank You

www.ingramcontent.com/pod-product-compliance
Lightning Source LLC
Chambersburg PA
CBHW080211170726
48282CB00030B/1072
* 9 7 8 9 3 4 9 1 7 4 2 8 3 *